OUTSIDE THE GATES OF PARADISE

A Poet's Walk through the World

ELENA VERONICA HALL

ISBN 979-8-88751-834-3 (paperback)
ISBN 979-8-88751-835-0 (digital)

Christian Faith Publishing
832 Park Avenue
Meadville, PA 16335
www.christianfaithpublishing.com

Printed in the United States of America

To Carmen and my wonderful husband, Christopher,
For their invaluable assistance, support and love.

Contents

Preface

The following is an eclectic collection of poignant poems compiled over a lifetime. As a child of the Cold War, I grew up fearing my world, a world of wars and atomic bombs and illness and poverty. Yet, I saw that this is also a world of great beauty, of deep love, and of unbounded compassion. There are flowers along with the missiles. There are lambs along with the wolves and dolphins next to the sharks. There are pristine waters along with polluted streams. And there are handshakes along with fisticuffs. This is a place where Jesus walked, loved, and died for us. He saw our world—the frightening state it was in—and wanted us to learn about it, learn from it, and write about it, even in rambling verses.

Mystic Jesus

Mystic Jesus,
The River of Life runs through your veins.

No sands had ever known your kingdom;
No star had ever shown your way—until that day.

You laid down your flesh as a carpet of suffering;
You showed us the bright path of righteousness.

Now the palms of your hands bear an eternal tattoo
Of love, faith, and redemption.

Lord of Love

His star lit up this world on that fateful day;
A caravan of knowing elders trekked along His way.
But He came from another, far distant realm,
Born to an Earth Mother, chosen by the Creator.

A special child of foresight and righteousness,
He was spared Herod's jealous, bloody wrath.
So many mothers sought Him for their daughters,
But He had a greater promise to keep.

If only they had known their own
When they sent Him to the cross,
For Jesus has the blood of every tribe,
Tried and purified by pain and unconditional love.

Immortal Beloved

I have stolen you from the Universe,
And I have claimed, claimed!
Every atom of your form,
And when they recombine,
Eons from now,
I will have you again—
Then all those who have become you
Will know how much, how deeply,
How infinitely,
I love you.

She

To Carmen

She walks through the wilderness
As if it were her kingdom—
A placid lake, a lone swan,
And reeds whispering in the wind.

While the strife of a cityscape
Beckons in the distance,
This is her home—
Solitude.

She walks along the paths alone,
Breathing in the scents of the earth.
She takes in, as a treasure,
Each tree, each blade of grass.

This wild refuge of nature
Knows her intimately—
Every thought,
Every dream.

It stays in her heart,
This magical place,
A haven of peace and tranquility—
Her own private world of sanctity.

The Alabaster Jar

To Mary Magdalene,
wherever her soul may fly
in the kingdom of heaven.

They had been arguing all evening.
Voices were raised to the rafters,
And fists were slammed on the table.
One said, "We should go this way!"
And another one said, "We should go that way!"
All was a vortex of chaos, confusion, and unrest.

Then she walked in—
With a veil hiding her beauty.
But the Rose of Sharon announced her,
And they made way for her.
She passed the brothers slowly and calmly;
Eyebrows raised at her audacity.

She went straight toward the Master,
With an alabaster jar,
Filled with fragrant spikenard.
She broke the seal of the jar,
And bravely cupped the costly oil
In her beautiful hands.

Their eyes met. And He consented.
Then she anointed Him:
First His head, then His forehead,
Then His shoulders.
Soon the room was filled to the brim
With the wonderful scent of peace and love.

But then wrath filled the brothers' hearts:
All were aghast and angry,
And began to murmur amongst themselves,
For they did not understand the holy ritual.
"Save that for the poor!" they cried.
"Why have you wasted this precious perfume?"

Then, with one stern look,
He silenced them all:
"Stand away from her and heed!—
She does this in memory of Me,
And so, from this day forward, it will always and ever be
In memory of her."

Sister Veronica
August 15, 2020

The Red Star

She had diamonds sewn onto her moccasins,
So that her feet shone as she danced.
Her red and silver tunic spun in the sun,
Like a shining whirlwind.

And as she whirled and whirled about the circle,
A spell of wonder was cast upon the crowd.
All were spellbound by her magical movements
To the steady beat of the tom-tom drums.

If she caught your eye, you were frozen in time,
Wrapped in a cobweb of love and rapture.
Only a great and sacred magic
Could set you free from her powerful grasp.

So many fell prey to her glittering gaze,
So many were lost in the land of love.
Some returned and some did not,
And some sailed on where time forgot…

The Nature of Love

Strange angel,
You wrap our hearts
In a web of emotions;
Helpless as a fly
Are we in your power.

You set the order of the day,
And we obey your plan—
To love the other forever,
To cherish the fleeting moments
That may never return.

So complex is the nature of love,
So merciless and fathomless,
So unpredictable and incomprehensible
Is this mysterious sentiment
That has us all in thrall.

2018

The Capriciousness of Love

The joy of love,
The pain of love,

The ecstasies of love,
The miseries of love,

The completion of love,
The loneliness of love,

The generosity of love,
The selfishness of love,

The happiness of love,
The anguish of love,

The bliss of love,
The desperation of love,

The tenderness of love,
The jealousy of love,

The eternity of love,
The fragility of love,

The pleasures of love,
The agony of love.

Oh, the capriciousness of love.

Sharitarish—a Love Song

O Sharitarish,
Why do you haunt me?
You lurk in my soul
Like a grain of sand
In the belly of an oyster.
The gates of heaven
Are closed to us,
Yet I cannot purge you
From my thoughts or my heart.

O Sharitarish,
How I miss you.
You are a ghost
I cannot touch,
Yet I long for your touch,
And the way you used to weave
Your hands into mine,
Or hold me close to your heart
When another ventured near.

O Sharitarish,
I have circled the sun ninety-seven times
In search of you.
Now my hair is gray,
And all my charms have left me.
My hands are veiny and gnarled,
Like an old crone's—
You would recoil in horror
If you crossed my path again.

O Sharitarish,
I am at my wit's end.
The fates have been cruel to us.
They poisoned you
When you were young.
They have robbed us of our youth.
That's why I ran away,
All those years ago,
For I feared for our children.

O Sharitarish,
My body is withered and wrecked.
My face is a map of sadness.
My eyes are rimmed with pain and longing
For a love that was stolen from us.
How shall I live in this universe now—
Tied to you and the kind
And generous one,
Who truly loves me?

O Sharitarish,
I've gone wild now,
And scatter pinecones,
Flowers and rocks
On the ground before me,
Casting my fate to the wind.
The birds fly over me in pity;
The ravens laugh and mock me,
And God shakes His head in the clouds.

O Sharitarish,
What is the answer to all this pain?
Our souls are linked forever.
I don't want to quarrel with God's plan,
But since we parted that fateful day,

I have knitted a thousand pearls,
And all of them with faulty knots.
No one can wear my old regalia,
For the moths have eaten through them.

O Sharitarish,
I've lost my way,
And all the lovely pottery you gave me
Has been shattered.
I will wander this earth
Alone in my shackles,
In the cold, dark prison
Of the fortress
I have built around my heart.

O Sharitarish,
Surely God in His goodness will be merciful
And allow me one day
To pierce through the thick veil of cobwebs
I have woven around my soul:
A web of weeping and longing for a lost love.
I pray that He who sits on the Most High
Will remove this immortal agony,
And let me see your shining face once again.
Yours now and forever,
Sharishara

The Tracks of My Soul

The music of my past is in my soul:
When my hips swayed,
When my neck swiveled,
And when my feet danced.

I am searching for my roots,
But they elude me, like my lovers.
Where did I start my journey?
Where is my home?

Is it in lush gardens,
Or sandy deserts?
Is it in snowcapped mountains,
Or warm rice paddies?

My mind keeps looking back
As I get farther and farther
Through the centuries,
And I see no trace of my family.

A cacophony of laughter, songs, and drums
Haunts me from the distance;
O beautiful Akhet-Aten,
Where have you gone?

I have landed my fragile sailboat
On unfriendly foreign shores;
The waves are rough, the fog is thick,
And I have nothing to hold on to.

O ancient Akhet-Aten
Point out the sun to me,
So that I may find my way back home,
And my place among the stars.

Chain of Love

I lost the golden bracelet,
The one you gave me long ago,
Through the slippery sands of time.
Somehow it slipped off my hand,
Or did I give it away?—
Because I couldn't trust you
With my other self, the lonely one,
The lost one I cannot cast off,
The one whose loving heart
Was ripped out and drowned
In the black cosmic tidal wave
That overcame our home.

Oh, our beautiful home,
Our wonderful happy home,
The big blue pearl, the lovely one,
The one of purple diamonds,
Ensconced in sweet and sonorous swirling clouds,
Where the wild geese fly as far as the outer ring,
Is lost to the Dark One forever.

If only this were not true,
But just the nightmare of a restless and longing soul.
If only, if only, if only, my sweet, strong prince,
I could see the sky in your eyes once again.
If only I could conjure you alive again from my dreams,
Like the Great Spirit did with our first Father and Mother.
Oh, my love, my love, my only love,
Perhaps that could save us both,
And bring us together again.
Until then, I am chained to your shadow,
The devil's will,
And his own damnation.

Ah Nee Mah, Nana.

The Cave

To Johnny Cash

Oh, my dear one, I lurk in a cave of lost love and loneliness.
It has been centuries since I have seen the light.
My love for you is deeper than the depths of Hades,
The center of this earth bears my footsteps.

For me, eternal love means eternal damnation;
I shall never see the sky in this cave.
What do you know about me?
Who am I, truly, a ghost or a person?

I hide my identity in a misguided body;
The darkness obscures my doomed plan.
God's punishment is my love for you;
It lives on in my heart and soul.

So many cruel years have passed for me.
I have no right to love this way.
The sands of time slip through the hourglass,
Turned over and over by a capricious angel of the night.

How do I rid myself of this longing and sorrow?
How do I climb out of this terrible abyss?
I could have love and happiness if I let go,
But I am chained to the confessional.

Oh, my dear one, shall I ever see the light of day?
Shall I ever ascend to heaven above?
The mirror reflects a horrid stranger now,
But I'll be back to love you again, and again, and again…

The Broken Tea Set

My soul finds rest in God alone;
my salvation comes from Him.
He alone is my rock and my salvation;
he is my fortress, I will never be shaken.

—Psalm 62:1–2 (NIV)

He had sent her a beautiful gift
From an exotic and faraway place,
Chosen with care and reverence,
One he knew she was sure to embrace—
But, alas, the minions of Wicked Fate intervened,
And broke the sweet token of love to bits
So that she could never receive it.

Even so, she would have loved
To have even the tiniest fragment
Of those precious broken bits
That the wretched minions
Of Wicked Fate had so cruelly swept away
Before she could ever get to them.
But, alas, it was not meant to be at that time.

And so, the waiting, weeping, and searching began,
Across deserts and oceans and continents,
Across planets, galaxies, and even whole universes.
Long had she waited to hear from him again,
But, once again, the minions of Wicked Fate intervened,
And the lovers were then parted
For a hundred long and tortuous years.

She prayed in her dreams,
She prayed to the Lord,
And when no answer came soon enough,
She then flung out her very body and soul
To the great and fearsome cosmic winds:
"Meet me tonight in dreamland," she cried,
"There, might my dreams come true!"

"Meet me tonight under the starry sky," she pleaded,
"So that I may, once again, see your eyes of blue."
And so, this lonely, heartrending, haunting refrain
Rang out into the skies, then to the heavens,
And across the universe divide,
Until an angel heard it and spoke to the Savior
About uniting the lovers once more.

Bundle of Dreams

She carried her bundle proudly,
And displayed it majestically,
Like a giant Pearl of Suffering.

And although many had asked for her hand in marriage,
There was only one soul, in the whole universe,
Who could truly make her happy...

Sister Veronica
December 15, 2016
"Experiment Perilous '44"

Stolen Love

To Praetorius

Stolen love—
Sealed in a diamond teardrop,
And you said:
"I'll be back to steal you once again."

I left my silver breadcrumbs
On this planet and that,
But I did not see you
In this universe.

I was wrong to walk away from you,
But hell's fire was at the gates,
And now I spend my time without you—
In a purgatory of stolen fates.

Sister Veronica
October 24, 2016

The Purple Diamond

To Prince Rogers Nelson
(The Purple One) RIP

I asked God
For my true beloved,
And He sent me
A purple diamond,
On spiderwebs,
Outside my bedroom window.

April 21, 2016

The Kite String

It's all right to think warm thoughts
About someone you loved and lost,
For it's just a tugging on the kite string
Of love and destiny.

Kleis

To Ms. Maria-Elena Font
and her constant loving friendship

Her tiny feet slip across this world unanchored.
She has cosmic dust on her fingertips and in her hair.
She has butterfly wings, cat eyes, and far-reaching feathers.
The winds weave her lacy dress with flowers and leaves.
Her house is made of spiderwebs and clouds.
She flies on the radiance of sunbeams.
The moon gilds her path on the waters.
The wilderness is her playground.
Whole forests bend to her will.
Her tears water the gardens.
Her laugh spurs the birds to music.
She cradles all of life in her tiny hands.
She lives for love…
How far has the ribbon of light in her heart traveled?
Where else has she graced with that flashing smile?
We can only glimpse a trace of her gossamer trail
On a black velvet night of starlight and dreams.

Penelope's Web

There once was a little girl from the ancient land of America,
With very long, dark, wavy hair,
And pretty brown skin,
The color of gingerbread,
But only when she went out into the sun,
Because, otherwise, she was very pale,
And known as a Blessed Snow Face,
Which only happened when
The weather changed toward a very cold and long winter,
Which it normally did every once in a while,
So that people could learn to travel
Not only to different places on the earth,
But also to other even more interesting places in the universe.

Along with this strange and changing countenance,
This curious and adventurous little girl
Had bright sparkling eyes
With a ring of golden light in them,
A gift from her father and mother,
Who, like her, loved everything
And every single person
In the whole wide world very dearly,
And were very grateful for what the
Great Holy Spirit had made for the families of the earth.

So much did this magical little girl
Love what the Great Holy Spirit
Had created around her
That she wove little bits of it
Into a great big dreamcatcher,
Because she knew, frightfully,
Since the day she was born,

That a great and terrible sadness,
And the most despicable of abominations,
Were to come to all the Sacred Lands,
And to all the Sacred Peoples
Of this incredibly beautiful planet
Called Earth.

Then when the horrid Winds of Fate
Were about to blow the dreamcatcher down,
And destroy everything that was on the planet,
She gathered the many parts of it,
And all the things she had collected over the years,
And gently placed all of them
In her most sacred dreamcatcher box,
Where she kept all her most personal and private things
Until the day she would need them
To start life on the earth once again.

Sister Veronica

Cup of Christ

To Teddi

You were born,
Suffered and died
For this world.

You measured us
With your rod,
And found us lacking.

You guided us
With your staff,
But we did not follow.

You gave us
Your body and blood,
But we forgot your sacrifice.

Now the Cup of Love
Is far away from your sheep,
And we are lost without you.

Pilate and Procula

"Pay the pipers, Pilate,
And the harpists!" she says,
When I walk in, exhausted,
After such a long campaign.

"And don't harm that man
Everyone is talking about.
I've had a very frightening vision
About Him.

"He appeared in my dream
As a golden apparition,
Then as a man,
With stars in His eyes.

"He was pale and gaunt,
And very troubled.
He looked out at the crowd
With a tortured gaze.

"It was as if He carried
The weight of the world
On His shoulders—
And great pity in His heart.

"Oh, Pilate, my dear husband,
I beg of you,
Don't harm this man,
I'm afraid for you!"

And so, I did what she asked,
As I always do,
And tried to reason
With the mob around Him and me:

"I have found no fault
In this man," I said.
"He has committed no crime
That warrants death."

But they shouted violently,
And raged all the more,
And cursed this man,
Saying, "Crucify Him! Crucify Him!"

I pleaded three times
For this strange man's life,
But they ignored me,
And threatened to tell Caesar.

Thereupon I freed the thief
They loved so much,
And washed my hands
Of this innocent blood.

The Son

God peers at the world through the sun's eye—
A lens to look upon every soul.
What joy to see our shining light!
What pain to find us in disfavor.
The universe records our deeds and sins.
Oh, that the light would save us from ourselves
As His Son did!

Sister Veronica
January 30, 2018

Lotus in the Desert

Who is this being—
The Creator?

He placed us in a garden,
Yet we rejected His Word.

He flares His nostrils,
And we cower in fear.

He floods the world,
Then mourns His deed.

He sends plague after plague,
But we fail to heed.

He sends us manna from heaven,
Yet we plead for meat.

He sends us His only Son,
And we hang Him on a cross.

He loves, forgives, and saves us,
Yet we fail to see,

We are both a thorn in His side,
And a lotus in the desert.

The Rose

O precious rose,
You hold the glory of creation,
The color of love,
And the fragrance of life.
Only your thorns separate us
From the sweeping pendulum of the cosmos.
Whose magnificent mind created such precarious beauty?—
A perfect balance of true nature.

Sister Veronica
July 9, 2018

She Offered Her Hand to Me...

To Simone

She offered her hand to me in my distress.
Instantly, we were friends.
Many times over after that, she came to my aid.
Oh, bless the hand that reached out to me in my time of need.
Now and forever will she be my friend, and those hands,
Everlasting, lovely, and blessed by Jesus the Christ, our Savior
—Who gave up His own hands for us.

NB: She spoke no English, but her hands did.

No One Could Have Known...

To Natasha

No one could have known
An angel was among us—
That Jesus had sent her in His name,
And that she would continue His work.
She washed my feet gently and sweetly;
How could my time be more blessed?
And then I washed her feet, gently and sweetly,
—and then laid myself to rest.

Celtic Samurai

To Christian

Celtic Samurai!
How did you get such eyes?
Red and gold strands in your hair?
Is it that you are from another realm,
Somewhere yet unknown?
Those dark mercurial eyes tell a story.
Is it a long-lost love?
Amber flows in your veins—as a
New life force has taken root.

A German-English Rose

To Tatjana

There once was a German-English rose,
And the whole garden felt her peace and repose.
Then one day, a busy little bee came along
Jumping wildly around with his dances and song,
And not seeing what Jesus had really meant:
New roses, all kinds, and mixed-up ones too,
Are all part of Him and from heaven sent.

"Imagine heaven forever," a message from Michael,
who turned to me and showed me his cross.

The Last Flame of a Candle

To Ardip

And she said that her name meant the last flame of a candle—
Raptures of wonderment rang in my soul at that.
Did her father know when he chose that name
In the Holy Book, just how much
Pleasure, kindness, and joy she would bring to the world?—
Especially to ill strangers like me.

He Washed My Feet...

He washed my feet,
Then I washed her feet,
Then she washed my feet,
Then I washed His feet...
Now we shall all wash our feet
At the foot of the cross,
Forevermore.

A Song to the Virgin—a Woman's Prayer

O golden-eyed Mary,
Rose of Sharon, who walks in grace,
Once a virgin for the human race,
Bearer of the Christ-Child,
What evils befell you on the road to love.

O golden-eyed Mary,
How you were afraid for your baby!
They, who hounded and hunted your infant,
Dishonored, defamed, and disparaged you—
They, who never knew their king.

O golden-eyed Mary,
The sweet feelings you felt as your belly grew,
That a Star-Child from God Himself was due,
Kept your face from showing trepidation and fear
To those at Herod's evil bidding.

O golden-eyed Mary
The Chosen One,
How you held your beautiful head up high,
And walked through the hills and dales of the desert,
Plagued by dangers, deceit, and treachery against your holy babe.

O golden-eyed Mary,
Confident, brave, and righteous woman,
We are your daughters.
We weave your heavenly trousseau with gossamer strands of gold,
And the delicate scents of spikenard and myrrh.

O golden-eyed Mary,
We adorn your gown with pearls of every shade,
And fasten your sandals with the most tender palm leaves.
Your violet veil is a gift from the Holy Spirit herself
To protect and shield your sacred heart.

O golden-eyed Mary,
Your blue cloak we take from the sky
So that the sun will know where to shine;
And we arrange the stars on your evening dress
So that the Christ-Child is watched over from the heavens above.

Sister Veronica
2016

The Blue Flame

To Captain Eric Weuve—"Xerxes"
Station 64 Orange County Fire Department
Westminster
December 14, 2016
RIP, Semper Fi

A beautiful, majestic hawk
Sat at the edge of a gaping canyon,
Wondering whether to take flight across it,
When suddenly a great and shattering earthquake
Shook him off his lofty perch.

Down he tumbled,
Past the red rock cliffs,
Unsteady and unready for the winds of fate;
He had but to hope and trust
In the Great Spirit to save him.

As he fell toward what he thought would be certain death,
A bright blue flame, that looked like a huge arm,
Came along out of nowhere,
And carried him away, across the canyon,
To the other side—to await his lady love and family.

To the Keepers of Paradise—Aphrodite's Lament

O Zephyrus!—Sweetest of winds!—
Whose pure and gentle strength whisked me to this earth—
Your tingly breezes carry perfume,
And fill my heart with joy and mirth.

O Zephyrus!—Blow caresses through my hair!—
And chase the clouds away!
You bring the essence of spring air
As I watch the pretty winged ones play.

Dear Goddess of Love and Beauty, whom, by my own breezes,
I ushered pure grace upon land,
I fear for you I cannot oblige, nor do for you my duty,
For I have been so fouled by the blindness of man.

No sweet essence penetrates
The darkness of my shroud.
As my little friends drop from me,
I am but a black and ugly cloud.

O Poseidon!—Master of the abundant oceans!—
Take me riding in your dolphin-drawn chariot!
Let me bathe once again in the foam that begot me motion!
Gather the creatures of the seas with your lariat!

O Poseidon!—Let me eat and drink of your endless bounty!—
Let me cool my body in your liquid mirror lakes!
Let me cleanse and refresh my beauty!
Let me play amongst the waves and whale wakes!

My dearest Golden One, though I was your midwife,
I have since lost my splendor; I am murky and on the wane.
I can yield no creatures; I can yield no life.
I beg you, never enter my poisoned domain.

Once pristine, I am all but dead—
A stagnant pool of death.
Unlike the mighty Styx I bred,
Not a soul dare take a breath.

O Glorious Golden God Apollo!—
Who comes from the night with rosy Eos—
Bow down your crown so I may follow,
And worship you, my brilliant Helios!

O Apollo!—You, the giver of light to life!—
All things are aglow with your friendly fire!
Warm my heart and make things ripe!
Play for me your golden lyre!

Beauteous Aphrodite,
Alas, I cannot shine for you.
My beams on earth are deadly,
And my lyre notes are few.

My rays, though yet invisible,
Would harm your lovely face.
Hide from me, I beg you,
My glory is disgraced.

O Artemis!—Take me to your woods!—
To your forests ever green,
Where birds sing symphonies for the gods,
And maples gush nectar honey-sweet!

O Artemis!—Let us search for brave Adonis,
Who hunts the fiercest of your game!
We could race with Atalanta,
Or hunt the wild beasts of the plain!

Sadly, dear Aphrodite,
I'm afraid we'll never play.
I, the quintessence of chastity,
Have finally had to pay.

A rain of acid stripped my maples,
And my beasts are in the past.
Silence has replaced the music of the birds.
As black snow blankets all, I am soiled at last.

O Zeus! Almighty One!—
Take me to Olympus, for here I cannot stay.
The keepers of our paradise
Have thrown their world away.

To My Love, Christopher

Could God have created another son?
He knew me before I knew him.
Riches would never hold me.
Instantly we were wedded.
So much water lies under
The bridge of our love.
Oh, if I ever wandered too far from you,
Please, forgive me, my dear one.
Heaven awaits us, and
Ever and always, our souls
Reunite.

St. Christopher

The green-eyed knight walks the realm of bygone days;
His large feet cover desert sands and boggy trails.
He has thunderbolts on his sandals,
And his red chariot flies like the wind.

But this place has long been abandoned;
The great deeds have been chipped out of the record.
The pillars, arches, and bridges are faulty and falling;
The pools and wells are poisoned once again.

Onward he voyages, across the world and back:
His breast is heavy, his brow is furrowed,
For this world will not comply—
It breaks the laws of heaven.

How many floods will he have to cross?
How many babes will fill his arms?
Alas, he cannot save them all,
And leaves them to the Creator's Son.

Sister Veronica
2016

Star Child

She walks on snakes and sleeps with wolves,
The jaguars and cheetahs visit her dwelling in the night,
She swims with crocodiles and manatees,
And plays with dolphins and sharks.

The rocks call out her name as she walks by,
"Pick me, pick me," they cry, in hope.
But now she rests in the pose of her ancestors,
Crossed hands, crossed feet, crossed fates.

She searches the heavens with questions,
Because the earth has lost its balance.
She gets her answers on the winds,
And teaches through stolen whispers.

She longs for the eyes her father made for her,
The violet ones, with a yellow ring as bright as the sun.
She wears her tribes on her wrists like shackles;
Her purple robe is worn and tattered from traveling so much.

She still wears the diamond teepee on her finger,
An unbreakable token from her beloved.
The rings of Saturn hold it together,
And all the stars of her ancient family.

She waits for the truth and nothing but the truth,
But it does not seem forthcoming in this wretched place.
The reluctant warriors are throwing up their shields and spears;
Soon they will defend this place no more.

Too many tears have been shed for it,
Too many rivers of blood and poison.
The time is coming to leave this earth,
And music and poetry and love will be no more.

And all that will be left will be spirals on the sands,
And the imprint of her crown in the dirt,
And her worn-out moccasins,
And the starfish and nautili, if there are any left.

Sister Veronica
2016

The Diamond Teepee

A diamond teepee holds the spectrum of this place called Earth.
A prism of the past is painted in the rainbow.
The elders know its secrets and fear it.
But keys to the future are in the ribbons of light,
When the apex of man exceeds the sins of the past.

Earth 2018

A suffering blue pearl
Floats in a breathless black sea,
Chained to a star and barren worlds,
Yet a place of great beauty and bountiful life.

A speck in an arm of a crowded galaxy,
It has vast riches and resources beyond measure.
But it sits alone and forlorn in a forbidden zone,
Cut off from the rest of the universe.

A pernicious plan has it in thrall to discord and death;
Crippling wars and mass destruction chip away at its luster.
Beings of light are trapped in the dark maze of a mad disrupter;
A jealous angel has wreaked his revenge on a divine creation.

The Father of All sent His only Son to correct and save this world.
Alas, they hung Him on a cross and disparaged His name.
What hope has this lost and far-flung paradise for redemption?
Shall it remain a prisoner of its own devices forever?

Humans 2018

Echoes from a past earth reside in our blood.
They whisper in our dreams from a higher plane.
Would that we could heed their loving admonitions;
Would that we could be spared their folly and woe.

The ancient life force of our mortal shell goes on and on,
Indifferent to the lessons of bygone days.
Caught in the cobwebs of our broken ancestors,
We reach in vain and war with new brethren.

If only we could discern the subtle teachings in our souls;
If only we could grow beyond the husk of certain death,
And strive to correct that which holds us back
From reaching the true hope of our Divine Creator.

The Red Swan

To the inimitable Maya Mikhailovna Plisetskaya
RIP May 2, 2015

"Oh, look," she said, "at that swan in the distance,
The silvery-gray one, way over there, all by herself—
So far away from the others,
She seems somewhat lost and forlorn.

"What a strange-looking creature!
See, there's an odd streak of fluffy red down
Running across her back, like a shawl.
Why, in all my life, I have never seen such a swan.

"So different is she, so cool and aloof,
Yet graceful and diffident.
She doesn't splash about to bathe,
Or force her way across the pond.

"She doesn't groom her feathers,
Or mingle with the others.
She seems like such a lonely little thing,
Gliding silently to music only she can hear.

"Her soft gray head tilts proudly and decidedly away
From the chatter and clatter of the gaggle.
So serene, so pensive, and confident is her gaze,
As if she's contemplating a secret journey.

"But now her eyes have caught the fire of the sunset;
How they glisten with a joy so private, so secret—
It's a happiness all her own.
Oh, look, she's coming towards me!"

The Mirror

Consider the ravens: for they neither sow nor reap;
which neither have storehouse nor barn;
and God feedeth them:
how much more are ye better than the fowls?

—Luke 12:24 KJV

That which casts a shadow,
What is it anyway?
What is the true nature?
What is the true form?
Matter against matter?
Or light against light?
Or matter against light?
What has the upper hand?
How is the shadow thrown—
That darkness against the wall,
The street, the cliff—
That crooked copied shape that lasts but seconds?
Who marks it?
Who took that strange, inconstant photograph?
Who holds the negatives to all those shadows?
Does the rock paint the hawk
That flies across it?
Who is that strange painter?—
The one we cannot see?
Yet, He sees us.

We cast a shadow, but does He?
His realm has shadow and light.
What lurks in the dark matter
That we are pinned against?
Cosmic mud, silt, or water?
The black waters:
Who or what marks their shadows in the deeps?
What or who looks inversely at us?
What is the true nature?
What is the true form?—
Flesh or fantasy? Or love?
It is but three little words.

2016

For the Love of Phaon

O Phaon! Phaon!
Don't ignore me!
Ferry me to the deeps
At least once more.

It's not fair for you
To be so handsome and kind.
I'm half-crazed for you,
And going out of my mind.

I promise not to tempt you
With adulterous love.
You can keep your life,
And your heaven above.

Oh, give me a chance, my darling Phaon,
To see your bright face at least once more,
And then you can cast me aside forever and ever
To the sands of a far-flung shore.

Black Sludge

Black sludge came up and spoke to me
In words of such perplexity:
"Must I choke you with a stench so foul?—
Don't you know where you are now?"
In hell it seems with bedlam near:
No drop from heaven,
No bead from fear.

The Purple Dolphin

Oh, the freedom, the freedom!
Of soaring through the sea!
Oh, the joy, the utter joy!
Of leaping in the air!

I run along the whale wakes,
And send my cries and songs
To the deepest part of my realm,
To the haven down below.

Oh, how I wish, how I wish!
That they above, that they above,
Could see my magical secret world,
My universe of love!

Then they would know, they would know!
How precious, how very precious,
Are the oceans, lakes, and streams
On this blessed place called Earth.

Teepees in the Snow

To Vova

Far away,
Across the world,
My fathers are drumming,
My mothers are dancing,
And my children are singing.

Far away, across the world,
Where the corn doesn't grow,
There are teepees in the snow,
And a darker turquoise,
And pines that look like cactuses.

The Navajo

To Dennison and Jan

He wears the stars of his people
In his eyes and on his heart.

His silence conveys the wisdom
Of a million crystal visions.

The ancient ones guide him
In this world and theirs.

He sculpts the symbols of the universe
On his jewelry and clothes.

He sees beyond the grace of dawn
And the infinite peace of twilight.

More precious than jewels are to him
The dew on spider webs, the cactus, corn,
and a stray feather on the ground.

He knows the subtle shades of snow,
And the perfume of the earth after rain.

He climbs the steps of the heavens
On sunbeams and moon-glow.

He knows that the earth
Has neither walls nor borders.

He forgives the cruel and the sleepers
With endless generosity and love.

The sheep, the bear, and the wolf
Are his closest relatives.

He harkens to the symphonies of birdsong
And the chorus of coyotes in the night.

He can sense thunder in the drums,
And the sky in a blue butterfly.

He is privy to the secret whispers of the pines,
And the silent tears of the mightiest eagle.

He feels the Creator in everything he touches,
And knows that the afterlife is just the beginning.

The Wave

To Nikolai Stepanovich Gumilev
1886–1921

I suppose it was there,
In the distance,
A small but beckoning rain cloud
In an otherwise
Brilliant sunny day.

And I had many sunny days,
And I was reckless and proud,
So reckless I never saw that cloud,
Nor any other kind of warning
That a storm was on its way.

I lived in the bloom of life,
Guided by a clock made of roses,
With no thorns to prick me,
Never looking forward,
Never looking back.

Suddenly it appeared,
Not a storm cloud, but a tidal wave!
It had been rolling itself backward,
Gathering strength all the while,
Only I didn't see it coming.

Then it washed over me,
Taking with it the very essence
Of a life that had held me in thrall
All those wonderful years,
All those wonderful years.

Now I sit on the beach alone,
Naked, old, and cold,
All my dreams and aspirations
Crushed and washed away
With the black and lonely tide.

Sister Veronica
September 21, 2018

The Butterfly

O Butterfly,
Fragile beauty,
With your delicate wings,
You fly on the winds of fate.

You have but a day or two
In this crowded world.
Who ponders your short life?
Who wonders why you were created?

You face the harshest of winds
That blow you from place to place.
Have you a family to look after?
Or a lover perhaps?

O Butterfly,
Teach us the essence of life,
The freedom of flight,
And the courage to thrive on this earth.

The Mountain

O mighty mountain,
Forged from the fires of Hades,
You tower above man in so many ways.

Your heaving breast pierces the sky;
A crown of clouds swirls about your peak.
You stand majestic, impenetrable, inspiring.

We define ourselves at your feet.
Have we the courage and wherewithal
To conquer your slippery slopes?

We stand in the shadow of your glory.
We dream of looking down at the world,
And the thrill of the feat that awaits us.

Lazarus

O Lazarus, you were rescued
From the grave.
What did you see
When the light from Him
Woke you from eternal sleep?

What have you to tell us
From the other side of life?
How long have you walked
The sands of this universe
Since then?

We await your bright countenance!
Your escape from the abyss of death
Was a miracle of the ages—
An infallible power bestowed unto you
Everlasting life.

Sister Veronica

Bird of Truth

The Bird of Truth soars in bloody skies—
How hard it is to fly in poisoned winds.
Yet, it is there, hovering above us,
Holding the olive branches in its claws
And forgiveness for the breath of death
In a beautiful world called Earth.

Sister Veronica
2018

Night

Night unfurls over the sky as a black carpet,
Sprinkled with sparkling diamonds.
All below bow for hours in silent homage
To the glittering majesty arcing above.
A different life flourishes in the darkness.
Creatures of the night reign in the cool veldt.
But too soon comes the dawn
With its ineluctable beams of godly light,
Mercilessly forcing her quick retreat,
And the glare of day once again
Hides the sacred secrets of the shadows.

This Mossy Rock—A tribute to Phillis Wheatley (1753–1784)

To the golden soul of Ms. Phillis Wheatley
and whatever realm it may grace again.

We are but guests upon this mossy rock,
So waterlogged and parched in places:
Though anchored to its generous harbors,
We are tied to *its* celestial destiny,
Held fast for a time by a glowing plaything
Of "the thund'ring God,"[1]
Which will itself one day implode
And cast adrift the germs of wretched creatures,
Who had not the sense—the "Imagination!"—
To look for other mossy rocks,
Waterlogged and parched in places,
And "with new worlds amaze th'
unbounded soul."

---

[1] Phillis Wheatley
Selected Writings
Poems on Various Subjects, Religious, and Moral (1773)
—from "In Imagination"

"Imagination!
Who can sing thy force?
Or who describes the swiftness of thy course?
Soaring through air to find the bright abode,
Th' empyreal palace of the thund'ring God,
We on thy pinions can surpass the wind,
And leave the rolling universe behind:
From star to star the mental optics rove,
Measure the skies, and range the realms above.
There in one view we grasp the mighty whole,
Or with new worlds amaze
Th' unbounded soul."

Where Have All the Children Gone?—a Song of War

After Marlene Dietrich's rendition of "Where Have All the Flowers Gone" (1963)
A folksong by Pete Seeger and Joe Hickerson

Where have all the children gone?—
Where were they taken?
Where have all the children gone?
It's been too long!

Masked men had snatched them quickly,
Then beat them one by one,
Then killed them all together, each and every one.

Where have all the mothers gone?—
Where were they taken?
Where have all the mothers gone?
It's been too long!

Masked men had snatched them quickly,
Then raped them one by one,
Then killed them all together, each and every one.

Where have all the fathers gone?—
Where were they taken?
Where have all the fathers gone?
It's been too long!

Masked men had snatched them quickly,
Then burned them in a cage,
Or hung them on a cross, each and every one.

Where are all the grandparents?—
Where were they taken?
Where are all the grandparents?
It's been too long!

Masked men had killed them quickly,
Then left them all in heaps,
Along a dusty road, each and every one.

Where are all the relatives?—
Where were they taken?
Where are all the relatives?
There's no one home!

Masked men had killed them quickly,
Then piled them all together
In mass graves across the world, each and every one.

Where are all the human souls?
Where were they taken?
Where are all the human souls?
Where have they gone?

Our Savior saved them quickly,
And sent them all to heaven,
Where they will live forever, each and every one.

Moonglow

Oh, beautiful, shining white orb,
The sun's mirror in the black of night,
You stare down coldly at this world,
Indifferent to its wily ways.

Would that we could be as placid as you.
Would that we could know the secret of your peace.
What have you seen in times gone by?
What cautionary tales are buried in your barren sands?

There you sit in the sky, piously high above us,
Showing and hiding your face,
A silent witness to our growth and demise,
A cosmic clock ticking out our fate.

Mars

The red planet
Sits alone in the dark,
Ashamed of the huge scar
That lies across its once brazen face.
All that it once was lies covered in dust.

Tears of a life that thrived and strived
Seep through the shattered rock.
Now it is but a beacon of sorrow and regret,
A wasteland of vanity
And ignominy.

When shall our curious feet
Walk upon its suffocating sands?
When shall we be brave enough to know
The solemn secrets from the ancient ghosts
That haunt this vast and lonely desert called Mars?

Sky

Crystal blue sky—
Infinite pathway lit by the sun—
Whereto do you lead?
The darker realm also beckons.
When shall we take up that intrepid trek
To the outer bounds of the universe?
What awaits us beyond the bounds of this earth?
Are we brave enough to leave our shells?

Sister Veronica
February 5, 2018

All This for a Flag—in Loving Memory of September 11, 2001

In loving memory of September 11, 2001

We stood there all those uncomfortable hours,
In our uncomfortable shoes,
In our Sunday best.

We stood for hours over those two gaping holes,
And around that breezy field of daisies,
Before those broken walls:

And if we could not stand,
We leaned on our crutches,
And if we had no legs,
We sat in wheeled chairs,
And if we could not sit,
We lay in our coffins,
And if we had no coffin,
We rustled on the wind.

We all stood there together,
All those long, never-ending hours,
For a flag.

Inspired on September 11, 2011
Revisited on September 11, 2018

Lest We Forget 9-11-2001

If I had never been troubled before,
I surely am now.

If I had never spoken my mind,
I'm speaking it now.

If I had never stood against tyranny,
I'm standing up now.

If I had never fought against evil,
I'm fighting it now.

If I had never loved my country,
I'm loving it now.

If I had never been troubled before,
I surely am now.

Your Matrix

You were the genius of my heart.
You knew all my ins and outs.
You needed but to look at me.
You never had a doubt.

In your hands, my heart lay,
So delicate and brittle.
In your hands, my heart lay,
Encumbered by so little.

Now it stays enclosed
In a bed of thorns,
And never shall you mold it
As you please.

Oh, could you never see
How you made it mourn,
Never see my forest
For your trees?

Locked up tight from you forever,
There it shall remain,
And for such a loving heart,
That truly is a shame.

Cir. 1990s

Cinderella of the Ghettos

To Rose-Linda

Cinderella of the ghettos,
Who walks gently through the lepers,
Though your mind's engulfed in shadows,
We remain your debtors.

The stench of the streets was your perfume,
The stalest port, your champagne.
While God has made your colors bloom,
We don't even know your name.

Now we shall have to buy your beauty
That shines through your haunting art,
For those eyes stare down our souls—
The reflection of your heart.

Cir. 1990s

Red Snow at Sarajevo

Three brothers,
Who want to be apart,
And the bombs that separate them
At the marketplace—
Red snow everywhere.

But the children are bewildered
By the horror of it all,
By the red snow
That comes so suddenly,
For Saint Valentine knows it's not love.

And the children
Never understand
What kind of life this is,
What red snow is,
And why it comes so suddenly.

Three brothers,
Who don't want to be apart,
Who only want to play,
And the bombs that separate them
At the safe zone.

Now it's hard
To pull their winter sleds
Across a frozen field
Of tombstones—
Red snow everywhere.

Cir. 1990s

Beauty in the Beast

Beauty—can you survive
In a beast as fierce as this?
Though art is here, it's so obscure,
We know it's you they've missed.

The wars are here, but Helen's not,
This is not a place for gentle feet.
The gods have left us on our own,
Without a prize for us to keep.

Have our sweet imaginations,
Gifted to us by the muses,
Suffered through these condemnations,
Or succumbed to their abuses?

Have we missed what Homer saw?—
Or the thrill of Shakespeare's schemes?
Have we nothing to reflect upon,
No beauty in our dreams?

Of Blake and Byron and van Gogh,
And countless of their peers,
We'll look to them and someday know
The omniscient sorrow of their fears.

Cir. 1980s

The Whitewashed Tombs

The whitewashed tombs of the pharaohs of
doom are filled with gold and poison.
They house all the abominations of the earth.
The unholy priests of the Black Pyramid
pay homage to their idols within,
Hiding their horns and sores beneath long robes and tall caps.

The jackals, the crocodiles, the filthy scarabs, and the dirty birds,
Have swallowed their heads and enslaved them.
They think they will live and reign forever,
As the last of their humanity is shed like
the ancient Serpent's rotten skin.

Woe that their domes are spread across the earth and beyond—
Stone markers of their dirty deeds.
The Rainbow Serpent waits at the gates for sacrifice,
For the blood of their children and for all their souls.

But the Lamb is coming to scorch the earth,
And cauterize the wounds they have long inflicted on His people.
He will lash these fetid beasts with truth and justice
And present them at the feet of their true master.

Then the traps they had set for the innocents and believers,
The tortures, humiliations, rapes, and murders,
Will they themselves face in the cold, dark dungeons,
Which they created for the children of the Most High.

Sister Veronica
August 11, 2016

The Kingdom of Many Colors—a Story in Verse

To the glorious enduring spirit of an
eleven-year-old Native American girl,
killed by the cruelest and most heart-
less beasts of humanity for a pipeline of
cheap crude, over sacred lands.
RIP Ana—"Little Angel of the Buffaloes"
November 1, 2016

Part I

On the most dangerous day of that not forgotten time,
They bravely walked into the nests of vipers
That had been so carefully laid before them
By the outlanders on sacred lands.
In those nests were the most venomous of snakes:
The vicious vipers,
The spiteful coral snakes,
The rotten rattlers,
The diabolical diamondbacks,
And the deadliest of all—
The king cobras.

That particular day, the serpents and vipers
had not yet shed their skins,
And people were still fooled that they had indeed,
And indeed, penitently, repented of all their evil deeds,
And had changed their ways
And truly wanted peace and truth.

But this was the greatest lie of all,
For all the venom of the collective
(Who had been gleefully slithering in their despicable dens)
Had been saved up in the little ones,
Who they thought would bear the blame
For the most unspeakable and horrible
crimes the world has ever known.

Yet, what they hadn't realized—because
they never realize these things
In their zeal to punish the Great Human Race—
Was that the hawks, the doves, the crows, the pigeons,
and the sparrows had spoken and embraced,
Along with the roosters and the hens, the
butterflies, the hummingbirds,
The Society of Royal Dogs and Cats, and
especially the poor stray ones,
The buffaloes and various others of God's
creatures, including little bugs and spiders,
Had all come together at dawn that very morning,
For the watchful golden eagles had been on the highest treetops
That whole, terrible, frightful, and inauspicious night,
Making sure that the Kingdom of Many Colors was protected
From the greatest evil they would face in a thousand years.

Part II

Then the Great Chief, whose heart had been wounded
By the evil stingers of the most pernicious scorpions—
And other even more loathsome creatures and
vermin too evil to even mention by name,
And because they had changed their names so many times—
Rose up from his bed and raised his palms toward the sun
So that the light from the wounds of Jesus,
beloved of the Great Spirit,
And, indeed, the most compassionate earthborn person of all,
Would warm and heal him and give him
the strength to protect and lead
The many peoples of our Lord's long-lost nations
Back to their beautiful and loving Kingdom of Many Colors,
All united under one flag that just happened to
be red, white, and a most royal blue!

Sister Veronica
November 11, 2016

Lake Baikal

To Vova

The sun casts a golden shadow
Upon a slowly breathing lake;
It leads me to the permafrost
Of my beloved ancient home.

The teepees were aligned
With a secret set of stars,
When long ago I crossed over
To another warmer country.

I miss the fir trees and the pinecones,
And where I used to run with the wolves.
I miss the scent of campfires:
The burning wood and my mother's stew.

Oh, the bounty of Lake Baikal,
The myriad creatures of its cool waters!
So rare, so clear, so pure it is,
So filled with mystical healing powers!

I used to swim in my dreams
Through its haven deep below.
It is in concert with the earth,
And the corners of the Universe.

The glorious break of day
And the onset of a peaceful twilight
See their faces in the shining mirror
Of the enchanting Lake Baikal.

Tears for Aleppo

Oh, ancient, beautiful, beleaguered Aleppo!
How you have suffered through the centuries—
From a green and shining city on a hill
To the crucible of destructive, bloody, and jealous wars.

Now rivers of blood run through your graceful streets and avenues:
The world's marketplace boasts not the
brimming cornucopias of old,
Filled with spices and goods from the four corners,
But a venue for rapine, executioners, and masked slave traders.

Oh, that you had glittered, sang, and flourished once!
The Tower of Babel had nothing on you.
Now your kings and children are but starving, wretched ghosts,
And the vacant stare of survivors will
haunt their saviors to the grave.

The warriors of mammon are winning your ruins and rubble
As their thieves and minions smash or cart
away your precious treasures.
Alas, the sweet air of Aleppo is fouled with
the scent of spilt blood and poison,
But your enemies have spent more on
arms than the gold they covet.

Oh, piteous Aleppo, you had long learned
your lessons from ages past,
And would have shared your abundance with neighbors and friends.
But these men of greed, rage, and revenge are a different breed;
They don't drink the pure waters from the snowy heights.

In the distance looms a shattered Palmyra,
Whispering your fate on the dry desert winds.
The God of Israel, it seems, takes no pity on you,
As fire and brimstone destroy the last of your idols.

Would that He, Almighty, could forgive your
transgressions this one last time,
And strike the axes, bows, and arrows from
the infidels' destructive hands—
Saving some vestige of your former beauty and bounty,
And the darkened souls of humankind.

Sister Veronica
August 18, 2016

Apatin—to Our Lady of the Snows

In the back of my eye,
There is an island, lovely and true,
Where lions graze with the sheep,
Where a leopard will guide a giraffe,
Where seals and fish and bears unite,
Where rabbits are not afraid to run,
Where the wolf nuzzles the lamb,
Where the birds are not afraid to land,
Where the trees reach out and touch the sky,
Where the swans swim with snakes in the lakes,
Where the harshest hail falls like white rose petals,
Where the sunshine on a stream glitters like diamonds,
Where the heaviest snow flutters in the wind like fine soft feathers,
Where the deer greet Adam and his Eve once more...

Sister Veronica
December 4, 2016

85

The Holy Grail

O Lord, to thee will I cry:
for the fire hath devoured the pastures of the wilderness,
and the flame hath burned all the trees of the field.

—Book of Joel 1:19 (KJV)

Jesus wept for Lot.

And on that day, the Savior,
With Moses and Elijah beside Him,
Standing like three great gleaming golden stones,
Surrounded the everlasting font of love and life
That had lain among the blood and the soot and the ashes
All these long, painful, enduring centuries,
And surveyed all the death and destruction
That the deceivers of the Great Human
Race had wreaked upon the earth.

Such and so low was the deceivers' descent into depravity—
This faithless and perverse generation—
That evil was sweet in their mouths,
And mockery, derision, and sarcasm
Rolled off their tongues like honey.
There was no boundary they would not cross,
No limit they would not push against,
In their pursuit to punish and rule the world.

So nefarious, merciless, and cruel were the deceivers' evil plans,
So powerful, so pervasive, so impenetrable
Was the web of lies they had woven,
That practically no one could see or hear the truth
Until that fateful day when the heavens opened up like a great book,
And the moon and the sun stepped back into the blackness of space,
And a great and glittering white cloud
Descended upon the earth…

Sister Veronica
December 1, 2016
Revisited April 29, 2022

Ghosts of the Apaches

The coyotes are running wild with glee in the desert tonight,
But this time, it's not just by the light of the silvery moon.
No, now they are carousing in the bright sun of day,
Unafraid of the white man's gun.

"Lay down your rifles and invite them in,"
Said the wise elders of old.
"The Thunder God is what they fear—
Keep your friends close and your enemies closer."

Sister Veronica
August 21, 2016

The Black Widows

Step out of the web before it's too late;
It's all an illusion to seal up your fate.
The human soul is immortal and priceless;
Don't sell your life to the doomed unrighteous.

The widows of Baal are dressed up in death.
They pick your pockets and take your breath.
You will never be part of their One World Tower;
It's but your blood they need to remain in power.

Osiris the Great lost his star long ago,
And the jackals have eaten his bones.
All that is left is a coven of spiders,
Casting their webs deeper and wider.

Run! Run! Little ones, as fast as you can,
For the devil is coming for the chaff of man.
Step away quickly from the burning cross,
Lest Christ, our Redeemer, mourn your loss.

Sister Veronica
October 4, 2016

The Three Shoes

To the blessed victims of the massacres at the
El-Botroseya Church
aka St. Peter and St. Paul's Church Abbassia,
Cairo, Egypt on December 11, 2016; the St.
Mark's Coptic Orthodox Cathedral, Alexandria,
Egypt, and the Mar Girgis Coptic Church in
Tanta, Egypt, on Palm Sunday, April 9, 2017;
and several other massacres too numerous to list

The bells were silenced,
The pews were bloodied,
The icons were marred,
The crosses were burned,
The marble pillars were pitted,
Bodies and bones were pitted,
Bloodcurdling screams and wails rang in the arches,
As the dust of the martyrs whirled up to heaven.

Three ladies' shoes,
And bloodied children's clothes,
Were stacked on a scripture-littered bench in the corner.
A nun sobbed bitterly over the slaughter and wreckage.
A donkey brayed somberly outside the doors of the cathedral.

An assault on our Lord has taken root
In the holy land of His refuge.
A borrowed sacred duduk will not stop
wailing in blessed Egypt tonight.

Woe unto those who will not turn back from their evil ways:
For them, the portal to hell has been irrevocably opened;
Its gaping maw awaits its foolish prey.
The dead will return to the earth,
But their murderers will not.

Woe to the indifferent ones,
Who stand to reap and profit and benefit
From the sufferings of our Savior and His beloveds.
The dead will return to the earth,
But the mockers will not.

God help them,
But He may not.

Sister Veronica
December 11, 2016
April 9, 2017, etc.

Souls in Boxes—in Loving Memory of September II, 2001

Remembering the United States of America's
September 11, 2001

"Dein Sinn ist zu, dein Herz ist tot…"
[Thy sense is shut, thy heart is dead.]
Faust—Johann Wolfgang von Goethe

In the middle of the city of the peoples they conquered,
They built a great and glittering tower
With huge glass windows
That provided great views of their spoils.
They made toasts with champagne,
Ate hors d'oeuvres on gold trays,
And lauded themselves in long speeches at their victory celebrations
In their great glass tower,
Mocking the souls beneath it.

And then they charged large admissions
For a view from their tower;
They made museums of the horrors
And sold cheap souvenirs
Imported from a country of slaves.
For many years, they ignored the legs that no longer walked,
The lungs that no longer breathed,
The hearts that no longer pumped,
And the plights of the widows, orphans, and bereaved
In their great glass tower,
Mocking the souls beneath it.

They threw but scraps to the wounded survivors and rescuers
And diminished their day of mourning and tributes
With false honors, praise, and riches to themselves.

They laid lush carpets and held sumptuous feasts in their tower
For themselves, their guests, and their most faithful friends,
Who had helped them accomplish their most cherished dream.
They laughed and clapped and cheered at their
hollow victories all over the world,
While the gaping holes below them, those
vales of endless tears, gushed on
In the cold, foreboding air outside their tower—
mocking the lost souls beneath it.

But worst of all,
They ignored the desperate cries and pleas
From the thousands of boxes of ashes, which held in abeyance
The true scope of their lies and deathly, earth-shattering deeds:
Boxes of burned bodies,
Bones and dreams lay locked away,
And the ghastly truths,
Long hidden from the world, lurked silently
On the other side of the wall
Of their shining throne room in their great glass tower—
Mocking the lost souls beneath it.

Yet in all this time, they didn't see the shadow of the cross,
Nor the stars and stripes of hope and justice and freedom
That lay along the breadth and scope of their great glass tower,
That mocking, malicious monument to greed and power.
They didn't notice the souls rising gloriously
To the heavens from the ashes beneath it—
Because their minds were closed, and their hearts were dead.
God puts His angels in
Where humans fear to tread.

Sister Veronica
September 11, 2015

Turquoise Eyes Looking Down

To Olivia

Oh, my dear "Turquoise Eyes Looking Down,"
May I turn your heart from that wretched frown?

I have seen you, and you have seen me,
Do you not know you are so lovely and sweet?

You, my dear one, are a blessing from Jesus,
Sent from heaven to love and to teach us.

But with your gaze cast so low, we cannot see the light
That the Lord gave to you with all His might.

Oh, beautiful "Turquoise Eyes Looking Down,"
You are a beacon of life and of wisdom.

Show us, my dear one, the ocean you carry within—
That we may rejoice and become a true Christian.

Sister Veronica
October 24, 2016

Ode to Apollo

O powerful Apollo!
You light up this earth
With your blinding radiance,
Yet turn your bright face,
And we are in darkness.

Untouchable star,
We are enthralled
By your brilliance;
Tongues of ghostly fire
Rise from your surface.

Your winds have wings
That fly out to the cosmos,
But we are tied together
Beyond all understanding—
O catalyst of life in this world!

Generous Apollo!
Shine your bright face upon us!
We are beholden to you
For our lives and our future,
A gift of our distant Heavenly Father.

September 5, 2018

Anchor Boy and Moon Girl—a Story in Verse

Part I

To the Hopi and all their hopeful cousins all
over the world,
And especially to my husband, Christopher

There once was an American Indian princess,
the last from a very old family,
Who lived on the heights of what is known
in these parts as a "mesa."
Now a mesa was basically a small mountain
with a flat top instead of a pointed one,
That is, a mountain that is missing its peak
and looks somewhat like a table.

How this small mountain had lost its peak was
not known or investigated by anyone.
It was set like a jewel, deep in the expanse of a red and sandy desert,
Which it was said had once been a huge and bountiful sea,
But no one had any real proof of that either,
so the notion was never pursued.

Life on the mesa was harsh, difficult, and,
more often than not, very dull.
There were no forests, no rivers, and no trees of
any kind. In fact, its one saving grace
Was a gushing spring at its very center, which
bubbled up fresh water every day,
Providing all the water needed for drinking, for bathing,
and, most importantly, for growing corn.

Corn was the lifeblood of the inhabitants
of the flat-topped mountain,
And the spring always provided enough water to
produce a crop that fed the entire tribe
From a very old family, a family so old that most of
its distant relatives had long been forgotten,
Along with any other way of life, other than staying atop the mesa.

The reason for never leaving the confines of
the mesa was not really clear to anyone
Who lived upon it, but the fear of leaving it
had become so deeply ingrained
In the minds of its inhabitants so as to be a
sacred law, never to be broken by anyone
Who wanted to go to the stars and see the Great Spirit in the sky.

One day, our dutiful princess, the last from a very old family,
So old that many ancient relatives had been
already long since forgotten,
Happened to be walking very close to the edge of her world when
She accidentally dropped a basket, laden with
the last ears of corn before winter.

One by one, each ear of corn rolled helplessly
over the edge of the mesa
And down to the forbidden world below,
which was considered the absolute
Worst place anyone could end up, especially
those precious ears of corn,
Which would most certainly be swallowed
up by anything lurking below.

Not thinking of anything other than saving
the last ears of corn before winter,
Our last princess from the ancient family,
in her zeal for rescuing the corn,

Accidentally ran over the edge with the corn,
falling straight down into a pit
Of quicksand that had gathered at the bottom
of the mesa after many, many years.

The sand was so fine and slippery that she slid
right down through the middle of the earth,
Finally coming out on a completely different side of the world.
When she came to her senses, she realized
she was lost in a foreign land,
Far away from the flat-topped mountain and her
tribe, which she might never see again.

Part II

After crying and mourning her lot a bit, our
princess, now lost from her very old family,
Started to walk the hills and dales of the unknown
terrain in search of food and shelter.
She did find food and shelter, each of which was
not always fresh and not always safe,
And it cost her a great deal, sometimes great sums, called taxes.

Then when the last of the handmade jewelry
she was wearing when she fell
Through the earth had been sold or stolen, she
had to work as a slave and then a maid,
And then as a secretary for some mad magicians,
who loved money more than people:
They had the power to stir up and profit from
great wars and caused many a nation to fall.

This, she decided, was a terrible way of life, not even worth living,
So she walked away from that foreign land,
and on and on, seemingly to no avail.

And just when she was about to give up all
hope, she found an ancient path,
Which led to a rocky shore, which led to a
dark blue and far-reaching sea.

Now this was a truly beautiful place. Here, the
air was fresh, and the land was clean.
The sun was warm and bright, and everything
shone in the light of day.
All kinds of birds flew joyfully around; fish leaped out of the sea,
And the shore was strewn with seafood and edible weeds.

Our princess, however, had never seen an ocean before,
And, therefore, did not know the treasures
and bounty it brought to the world.
Starving, shivering, and mourning what she
thought was her miserable lot once again,
She sat on a flat rock on the shore and cried her very heart out.

In fact, the princess from the ancient family
cried so hard and so profusely
That her heart literally jumped out from
its normal place in her chest,
Flew past her lungs and esophagus and out of her mouth,
Finally coming to rest on a large flat rock that
was lying just a few feet in front of her.

"Well, that's it," she said with a long and resigned
sigh. "That was the last straw, I guess.
Life of any kind for me is over now. I'm finally
done for. I have given up the ghost.
I'm not even living anymore, and most telling and worst of all,
There is my very own heart, sitting on a rock right in front of me."

What a ridiculous and humiliating end, she thought to herself,
For a princess from such an old family, so old
that many of its ancient relatives
Had already been long since forgotten, and
now she, the very last princess
Of this very ancient family, would now most certainly be forgotten.

There was nothing to do for it but lie down and continue to weep
Until the water in her eyes would finally subside,
And she would shrivel up and eventually be washed off the shore
By this wave of salty water that kept coming
and going upon the beach.

So our princess from the ancient family, whose
relatives were mostly forgotten,
And who was herself about to be just as forgotten,
Turned over on her back and gazed up toward the sky,
Which, by this time, was a very dark blue
and filled with sparkling stars.

Part III

Then when she was just about to drift off into the sacred slumber
That takes one up to or far from (as the case may
be sometimes) the Great Spirit in the sky,
Who watches over the mesa and everything else in the universe,
Came a piercing cry in her vicinity: "Hey, miss, is this yours?"

Startled back to her senses, our princess from the ancient family,
Who had given up completely, and who
had almost been forgotten herself,
Suddenly rose up from the rock she was lying
on and tried with all her might to focus
On a tall dark shadow that was standing
just a few feet in front of her.

Thinking she was simply hallucinating
from the lack of food and water,
Our surely forgotten by now princess, from the ancient family,
Rolled over once again onto her back and said simply,
"Oh, just throw it away, I don't need it anymore. I'm already dead."

"Oh, no, you're not! You're not dead at all, miss!" said the voice
From the tall dark shadow. "Here, put your
heart back in its place, quickly!
It's still beating, see? Here, swallow it quickly, or you really will die,"
Said the voice from the tall dark shadow that
was now carefully bending over her.

"What? Swallow my heart? How can I swallow my heart?"
Said the confused and very weary princess from the ancient family.
"Yes, you must do it quickly," implored the
voice from the tall dark shadow.
"There's probably not much time left in it by now."

Never having had a hallucination before and
certainly never one that talked,
Our princess did not know whether to
obey the tall dark shadow or not,
So she just stayed quiet, waiting for the next
moment of incredulity to unfold.
"Here, miss, swallow it with some fresh water,
hurry!" pleaded the tall dark shadow.

Fresh water, having sounded pretty good
after many days without any,
Was a good enough reason, she thought, to
appease the annoying apparition,
Who seemed so intent on getting her coughed-up
heart that was lying on a rock,
Back into her wretched, starving, and shivering little body.

And so, after a few good gulps of some cool,
unsalted, and actually very sweet water,
Our princess from the ancient family also gulped
down the fleshy, still beating heart,
Which rapidly made its way down past her
esophagus and toward her lungs,
Immediately resetting itself in its proper place within her chest.

"Wow, that was close! It was almost too late for it to get back in,"
Said the tall dark shadow, who was by this
time gently holding our princess
From the ancient family (who had almost been just as forgotten
As those who actually were forgotten)
firmly in his strong, warm arms.

Part IV

"You know, you shouldn't leave your heart lying around like that,
You could accidentally kill yourself," said the
shadow with the strong, warm arms,
Who was by now wrapping our princess from the very old family
In a warm wool blanket that he had from the
time when he served on a sailing ship.

"I thought I was dead. Am I not dead then?"
Asked the princess from the very old family,
weakly and somewhat confusedly.
"No, you're not dead at all, and you're actually
kind of pretty too," said the shadow, shyly.
"What are you doing out here at night with your
heart lying on a rock on the beach?"

"I was dying, I mean, I was terribly lost and then I was dying,
Or at least I thought I was dying, and then you came along
And got my heart back in my chest with
that good-tasting water. Say,

What kind of water was that anyway? It was
so sweet, refreshing, and revitalizing."

"Oh, that was Living Water from the River
of Light," said the shadow,
Who, in the brightening dawn, actually turned
out to be a very handsome young man.
"The River of Light?" asked the newly
revitalized princess. "Where is that?"
"I can take you there," said the young man, but
the path is rocky, and it won't be easy."

"Oh, that's all right," said our now-not-forgotten-
at-all princess, "I'm used to rocky roads."
They then walked a good ways along the rocky shore, this
time hand in hand, for, at last, our newly saved princess had
started to trust him, the handsome young man. They soon
came upon a Beautiful island, filled with lush trees and flowers
and white sand that shimmered in the sun like snow.

"By the way, how did you happen to find me way
out here?" asked the not-forgotten princess.
"We saw your skeleton," answered the young man.
"You see, you are a very special person,
A descendant from our very ancient family, one so
old that no one had ever even heard of us, but
We know where every member of our family
is and rescue them wherever they are.

"I was once lost, too, and so was most of my very
old family. Almost all of them were lost
In a great flood, which washed away all knowledge
of our ancient relatives and all the things
They had made. This was most distressing for
those of us that survived this catastrophe,

But then we found the River of Light and learned
to fish in it. Later, we sailed on ships along it.

"We then sailed all over the world, meeting all
kinds of peoples from very old families too.
We even learned how to sail to the stars, but
not before much hardship and
Many horrible and destructive wars, which
left most of our very old family,
And many other very old families, either
destitute, dead, or forgotten."

"Hey, what's that thing in the middle of that
glowing river?" asked the princess,
Running up to what looked like a huge golden
anchor, set in the middle of a shining river,
Set in the middle of the island, which glistened
with every color of the rainbow.
"Oh, that used to be an old wooden cross, but now
it's our star, the bright 'Morning Star.'"

Part V

"The bright Morning Star?" gasped the princess,
her eyes glittering as she gazed upon it.
"I know that star. I used to see it in the mornings.
But how can a star be set in a river?"
"Oh, that's not just any river," said the handsome
young man, who had taken her hand,
"That is the River of Light, and whoever
drinks from it will live forever."

"Wow, that's incredible! But I'm not sure
I would want to live forever.
It was pretty rough the first time on this earth,
and people here were not always kind."

"Oh, but we are a different sort of people now," said
the handsome young man. "We are never cruel, selfish,
or violent. We love all peoples of the universe, and
we help guide them to the River of Light."

"Say, all this time, I forgot to ask you—
what's your name?" asked the princess
From the very old family, who was not forgotten at
all, and who was now going to live forever.
"My name?" said the handsome young
man with strange glowing eyes.
"Oh, it's very long and complicated, and I don't
think you or even I could pronounce it."

"I understand," said the princess, happier now more
than she had ever been in her whole life.
"Then, I will just call you, 'Anchor Boy,' so I will
never feel lost again." "Good!" said Anchor Boy,
"Then I will call you Moon Girl since that's where
I found your soul, shining under the moon."
"Would you like to go for a swim now?" asked
Anchor Boy, with a huge smile.
"Yes," said the princess from the very old family,
"and I think I could swim here forever."

The beginning.

The Flower of Life

The fragile Flower of Life hangs in the balance
As the earth sways away from its true path.
The organ wails alone in hallowed halls,
As we are deaf to its harmony and grace.

The Virgin of the Rocks[2] stays silent,
As do all the archangels who guard the Holy Font of Life.
Uriel looks on perplexed and impatient
As the songs of Orion echo in the distance.

The powers that be run crazed in the dark
To the bowels of this sacred heavenly sphere,
Where spiders cast their webs of lies,
And moles dig their holes for ill-gotten gains.

The ancient veil that covers the Portal of Knowledge
Has been pierced by eyes too blind to see.
The mouths of the secret caverns yawn in agony,
While the blood of the innocent is spilt in vain.

The finger of God leaves His mark
On everything before the human race.
Yet we are too greedy, too proud
And too arrogant to take up our Holy Place.

---

[2] After Leonardo da Vinci's *Vergine delle Rocce* (*Virgin of the Rocks*) (Louvre)

The folly of disparate agendas
Tangles this world in endless strife.
Can we shatter the mirror of our own faults?
Can we strive for the truth instead of riches?

And so, the mystery endures—we cannot reach
The Realm of Light while foraging in the dark.
The joyous music of the universe eludes us;
The mad clatter of this world obscures it.

Sister Veronica
December 11, 2018

A Plea to the Red Warrior

Part I

"Red Warrior! Red Warrior!" she cried aloud, half-crazed.
And in one unabated breath she pleaded:
"Oh, Red Warrior, won't you please come to rescue us?
Can you not pierce through the veil of time
To save us from the minions of the serpent?
They have taken over this world,
It is all sewn up in their pernicious Dark Web.
They have all our children in thrall
And prone to the chasm of death,
Those wicked mistresses of the Golden Orb.

"They follow the directions of the Horned One.
They cannot escape the scope of his dark cloak;
It envelops their hearts and minds and bodies.
He has given them a badge with his evil star as a present,
A worthless bauble they proudly wear around their necks
Like an albatross of doom.
They hold many souls in darkness,
They cannot see the light.
They will not let us go.
They will not repent.

"Please ask our Savior and the Great Holy Spirit to intervene,
For they are planning, once again, their
greatest, most heinous crime of all!
They don't see the scars on Mars from the past.
They don't see the wounds in His timeworn hands.
Oh, my love, my love, my only love,
It is lonely without you in this time of peril,
But I can bear it until you return, my angel.
I await the miraculous clap of your horse's hooves
Against the hallowed grounds of the cosmic dunes,
Where they once scattered all of us so long ago.

"I will wait for that most holy thunder and lightning in the sky
To break their strong tools
At the blast of Gabriel's trumpet,
The thrust of Michael's sword
And Raphael's command!
Beat your drums, my handsome one,
Against the winds of fate,
Beat them like the sacred tom-toms of old,
Like the pulse in the center of the universe,
For that is my heartbeat, held in abeyance for you!

Part II

"I will wait to trace the map of life on your warworn face,
I will wait to soothe away the angst from your furrowed brow,
I will wait to hold you and love you
completely, as the Great Spirit wills.
We share and revere the divine spark in our hearts,
So tear them down, my love, like those of Jericho,
Those wretched walls that keep us apart!
Tear down the impenetrable filthy fortresses
That protect the evil ones from their true future.
Tear them down, O beautiful Child of God,
In the name of the Father, the Son, and the Holy Ghost!

"Shatter their wicked temples of sacrificial blood, O Brave One!
Silence forever the horrible strains of pain and woe
From our weary minds and careworn hearts.
Until then, I will wait for you, my love, patiently,
For I see the crystal blue sky in your eyes in my dreams,
And I will sing for you, every day, your favorite song
That Solomon wrote for us so long ago.
Till we meet again in the arms of Orion,
On Love Mountain! I am yours forever!
Agape!"

Sister Veronica
December 9, 2016

The Curse of Cain

Cain! Cain! How many times will you
stab your brother in the back?
How many more centuries will you add
to your crimes and bloodguilt?
The rubble of your vengeance won't bury your lies
And the cries of the children and mothers
You've destroyed for oil and gold.

Cain! Cain! Have you not wandered and
squandered your birthright long enough?
You cannot graft your rotten seed into foreign mothers' wombs;
You cannot crossbreed a plant with one that will never bear fruit,
For your evil wombs are now barren forever,
And no angel will intercede for you.

Cain! Cain! Make peace with your brother before it's too late!
Repent before the earth is shaken by the Lord's mighty foot.
The fiery and fatal storms of Armageddon are coming soon
To wash you and your children
Down to the pit once and for all.

Cain! Cain! You will never receive the gold
and oil and luxuries you seek!
Your mercenaries despise you, and will not
return these blood-soaked lands.
Turn away from this heinous endeavor,
for the Lord is surely coming
And will manifest His own inexorable vengeance and wrath
So that the sons and daughters of Cain never walk the earth again.

Sister Veronica
September 29, 2016

Gail of the Golden Hair

Golden hair,
And kind eyes that peer into your heart and soul.
I will be there in the cosmos forever
Loving you.

In loving memory of
Gail Marie Johnson Miller
RIP April 23, 2022

The Hunt

The scent of passion
Is heavy in the air.
It leads you to the prey and things
Your soul won't dare.

Fix your eyes upon me,
And you shall see my will—
My fear will not release me
Until you break that will.

With darting looks for liberty,
I search, but to no avail,
So in your fervid clutches,
I'll scream a blissful wail.

Keeper of the Key

Keeper of the key,
Why don't you set me free?

My heart is in your prison,
Are you not lonely for me?

Cir. 1990s

The Three Crosses

To Gail, RIP

She told me
That they had broken into her house
And had stolen all her gold jewelry—
But they left the three wooden crosses from Russia
That I gave her long ago.

2022

From the Ghosts of Benghazi

In loving memory of those abandoned souls
still hovering above the ashes of Benghazi.

Blinded by the glare from their shining idol,

Every soul so benighted will bear its sin.

Now when the beasts of human error prevail,

Ghosts of human valor and virtue step in.

Hell unspeakable awaits the usurpers,

And all those who walked on the graves of the brave.

Zion still holds out its arms to its brothers—

In God shall we trust and never another.

November 7, 2012

The Broken Diamond

Upon her high and lofty perch,
Lady Freedom is in a cage:
The Triangle of Death—her prison.

She wears the Broken Diamond
As an albatross around her neck,
For its fractured prism skews the glories of the past.

Her starry helmet has dimmed and rusted,
And the eagle upon it has long since died.
The laurel crown she carried is battered and withered.

Her once shining shield and sword have been blackened
With the blood of shameless wars for profit and power.
The world, once at her feet, now lies in ruins and poverty.

Who whispered in your ear, O glorious virgin?
What asp has bitten your mighty royal breast?
To whom are you beholden, so sullied and so woebegone?

Guide you the warriors of freedom, or
the warmongers of mammon?
Will you now fall into the bottomless pit
with the maggots of old?—
Or polish once again your sword and shield
for justice, eternal peace, and honor.

Sister Veronica
August 26, 2016

117

O Jerusalem!

To the youngest victims of terror in the Holy Land:
Mahmoud Rafaat Badran, June 21, 2016;
Hallel Yaffa Ariel, June 30, 2016; and all those before and after

O Jerusalem!
First a young boy and now a young girl—so close but worlds apart;
Yet the hot, oozing blood on their chests is the same red shade.
A temple, a mosque, a church won't shelter them
From the bullets, knives, and bombs that desecrate this Holy Place.

O Jerusalem!
Rip off your headscarves, your yarmulkes, your fezzes, your turbans,
And hang your heads in shame.
The stench of evil sacrifice and mammon
Has reached the gates of heaven.

O Jerusalem!
The Lord has set His foot, His grave, and His everlasting seeds
In a place of quicksand and war.
Hang on to the pillars, the mountains, and the waters on high,
For an earthquake is coming to shake them
down with lightning and fire.

Sister Veronica
June 30, 2016

Schadenfreude

In the aftermath of World War II,
Two young grave robbers
Stood over their victims:

"Give me half of your country for the common good," said one,
While stripping a body
Of its jewelry and gold teeth.

"Give me half of your country and your soul
For the common good," said the other,
While wrenching a silver crucifix from the rosary of a dead priest.

Then the devil reached up and took his prizes too:
Two robbers with jewelry, gold teeth, and a crucifix—
All in the name of the common good.

March 13, 2014

Utopia

Up high in the sky, away from the fray,
Victory stood over her dream.

Kindling the flames of democracy, she threw
crumbs to the birds at her feet.

Raw meat she threw,

And Molotov cocktails too,

In an effort to win her prize.

Now it's all in ruins, burnt to ashes—

Even her marble pedestal and golden wings are
black with the blood of coal and oil.

February 21, 2014

Ode to the Star-Spangled Banner

In loving memory of September 11, 2001

I was asleep,
And I slept for decades,
Dreaming of something else,
While a star-spangled banner waved in the wind over me.
I slept in the shade of a beautiful tree,
And nothing could rouse me.

Then one day,
Out of the blue,
While I was resting
Under that beautiful tree,
I heard bombs bursting in the air,
And then I saw rockets' red glare!

Oh, there was a perilous fight:
Broad stripes of blood covered the land,
Bright stars of fire gleamed in the twilight.
When I felt brave and looked o'er the ramparts,
I saw that our flag wasn't anywhere.
Oh, God, what a terrible nightmare!

When I finally rose by the dawn's early light,
Soon did I learn of my terrible plight,
For that which was once so gallantly streaming,
Had been shed in the streets with the blood of the screaming.
Yet the absence of that which I had so proudly not hailed,
Gave proof through the night that my dreaming had failed.

Oh, say can you see that beautiful tree,
Or the banner that waved in the wind over me?
But the silence was still o'er the land of the chained,
And the hearts of a people so many had blamed,
For a land of the free,
And a home for the brave.

September 11, 2011

Old Glory

There are bloody stripes across a blank, white sky,
And the stars have fallen to the bottom.
Where are the loyal hues it used to fly in?
Where is the royal blue it used to sail with?

The scroll of heaven is rolled up;
The parchments of freedom are burned.
No hymns of brotherhood reach the rafters;
No bells ring out what should be heard.

Cacophonies of screams and shots
Have replaced the odes to justice.
Once again, the world is flat,
As the earth spins off its axis.

With a mocking grin and yellowed eyes,
The devil stirs his evil cauldron.
To the dregs they've drunk the cup of lies,
A fatal brew of gold and slaughter.

Sister Veronica
June 23, 2016

Cold Stars

Cold stars hovering above me
In the black of night—
So remote, so aloof, so pious.

If I could touch your fire,
I might not be so judgmental—
But I am fastened to the earth's plane.

Yet in my dreams I fly
The airless expanse with ease,
Collecting diamonds along my trek.

I long for the time when I can know your abode,
And smile back at my homeland
From afar.

Holocaust and Human Folly

"Will the world ever learn?"
Elie Wiesel (1928–2016), RIP

The plagues of *Night*[3] shine in the light of day.
The horrors of darkness creep out from the shade.
A blue sky smokes, and blood has congealed
On a flag "seven times cursed and seven times sealed."

No, they never learn, Elie, and they never forget,
The bloodletters of the human rut.
The butchers, the blind, and the geniuses
Are joined together at the crippled hip:

They stomp their bloody boots on the necks of generations.
They scorch the earth with their cruel abominations.
The virus of evil is in our blood,
With waves of pain and death and flood.

I saw the devil's own try to stick their claws in you.
I saw them try to steal your all-embracing light.
Oh, how they would have liked to drag you too
To their miry pit and hopeless plight.

---

[3] *Night* (New York: Hill & Wang) refers to the title of a 1960 English translation of a memoir written by Elie Wiesel on his holocaust experiences.

They leave their bloody traces upon the rocks of fearless ages,
They maim the youth at birth and mar the love in races.
They cajole and bribe and win and conquer,
Leaving plagues of death and sores of canker.

No, they never learn, Elie, and never seem to forget—
How long it's been since they set out
To ruin the seed and the great destiny
Of our loving God's humanity.

But you know how to climb the barbed wire,
You know how to escape that eternal fire.
Your hands no longer bleed, nor feel our pain,
They clasp together at heaven's holy reign.

Sister Veronica
July 4, 2016, Independence Day
The United States of America

Mistress of the Golden Orb

In loving memory of September 11, 2001

The Mistress of the Golden Orb had long cast her net
Across the four corners of the globe,
And she has captured all sorts of dirty birds for prey and duty.
She wears her crimes like jewels in a crown, blasphemy as her robe,
And the souls of her victims like the medals of her generals.
In her eyes, there is the reflection of that evil Tower of Power,
Built with bricks of pain and a mortar of bloody tears,
While its altar of flesh sacrifice, of the past and present,
Gleams like a bright-blue jewel in the light of day.

Fifteen Septembers mark the century of death and destruction,
And the Queen of Terror and Oppression seems invincible.
But on this day, the beast did give forth its sandal in her name,
And perforce made her kneel at the graves of the dead,
Before rising once again to steal the widows' mites,
And suck the life from their orphans with her deadly fangs.

Oh, would that our most glorious eagle,
Who flies swiftly by the rays of the sun,
Could come and pluck out this yellowed-eyed monster,
That has the children of the earth in her claws,
And send her back to the fiery pit from whence she came!

Sister Veronica
September 12, 2016

The Poisoned Apples

To the Brave, the Few in 2016
Semper Fidelis!

And the beast did set his cloven foot
To walk in front of the Lord's bravest that Holy Day,
With his dirty red bag of poisoned apples, broken toys,
And children's souls,
To mock them and Him once more...

* * * * *

And there lay, for all the world to see,
The dead head of the dirty bird they worshiped,
The foul, stinking, rotten carcass
That held the world in thrall
Was no more.

Sister Veronica
December 11, 2016

The Crooked Smile

To TN and AB,
And the holy ghosts of DL and AY,
For the "Dance of Pain and Joy"
On Russia's "Dancing with the Stars"

They were skating and racing along on the blazing Lake of Fire,
When suddenly, they slipped, perilously and fatefully,
Down into its fiery depths.
"Save us, oh, Lord!" they cried, "Save us
from this dark and miry pit,
For we do not wish to die but to live with You,
Our Blessed Savior,
In the love and light of the world, forever and ever!"

And then a crooked smile,
In the smoke-filled Soul of the World,
Broke through the wretched and wrecked body,
Like bold lightning in the darkest thundercloud,
Revealing the Great Face of Pain
That had for so very long
Borne so much of the world's suffering…

"Forgive them and receive them," He said—
"O Heavenly Father,
The children in rags and riches,
For they do now know,
Most certainly and unequivocally,
In spite of their deluded and wicked parents,
What they do."

Sister Veronica
November 27, 2016

The Five Hundred Millions

The Five Hundred Millions have the world in thrall;
It's carved on the pillars and it holds up the wall.
The nations can read the vile pledge in their tongues,
And for the sale of their souls, it's a paltry sum.

Satan's sons rob the babes from their graves;
They walk the earth in shades of gray.
The Moth of Death has eaten holes in its hosts;
It picks their pockets where it finds the most.

The evil intellect has grown dark from its roots,
With the Tree of Knowledge too long in cahoots.
And those longtime "champions of civil society"
Will choke on their beards in the time of sobriety.

"Invest in death and damn your fellow man!
Sew up their lives in this evil plan!"—
So goes the mantra from the pit below,
But the weaver of lies only echoes it so.

The time has come to face the light
Before the Lord steps in with all His might,
For the Five Hundred Millions have sold their lot,
To the ancient serpent in whose face is rot.

Sister Veronica
October 2, 2016
Revisited 2022

130

Curse of the Seventeens

To the victims of Flight MH17, July 17, 2014

Blessed is the one who waits for and reaches
the end of the 1,335 days.

—Book of Daniel 12:12 (NIV)

The catafalques rolled on without any souls,
And the mood was appropriately grim.
They were all in their places, all in lock step,
To present the facts of deceit.

Mighty is the power of dark fruit,
When it wields its cudgel on the doves of peace.
And blinded, their minions do all of its bidding;
They bare their bodies and bleed their offspring.

But the ghosts of the victims are still on the field,
And they are yearning for truth and their loved ones.
Oh, how the hearts of man have grown cold and indifferent,
And woe to the perpetrators of this infamous crime.

The sundial has been turned away from the truth,
And blame remains cast on the innocent.
But the markers are there on the lying centuries,
For eagles' blood does not wash away angels' tears.

Tight and taught is the web of lies and subterfuge.
Great nations have now done their part of the deed:
They have cleverly interred the screams and pleas of the dead,
And have abandoned their souls to the potter's field.

Yet the threads of death they have woven so tightly
Belong to the Kingdom of the Anointed One,
For what has long been buried shall at once be uncovered,
And what has long been hooded shall at once see the light.

Everlasting shame and ignominy will be the lot
Of all the players in this well-funded farce.
The earth has never known such a treacherous plot
That rivals the fall of the Dark One.

Oh, Wizard of Lies, you have long lost your glory,
And your haughty children have lost their way.
Show them your mirror before it's too late,
Show them the truth of your horrible fate!

Sister Veronica
2014

Golgotha 12/12/12

Save me, O God,
for the waters have come up to my neck.

—Psalm 69:1 (NIV)

Once again, they spread their errors in the world:

Barabbas is freed, and Jesus is flogged.

"A scarlet robe, a crown of thorns, and a staff for Him!" they jeered,

"Mock Him, spit on Him, strike Him again
and again," roared the multitude,

And then they crucified Him, once again,
at the "Place of the Skull."

"Eloi, Eloi, lama sabachthani?" He cried—[4]

And a thunderbolt struck the earth.

Sister Veronica
December 12, 2012
Times Square, New York City

---

[4] From Mark 15:34 (NIV)

A Laurel's Lament

Oh, Wisest One,
Why have you left this obsequious leaf in the wind?
Fate always has its reasons,
But soon this frond won't bend.

There is no more room for gentleness,
No more room for love.
Man's warm blood has turned to frost;
It's left him cold and left me lost.

Ugly sneers and evil eyes
Have replaced their once cherubic smiles
As hellions spread their vicious lies,
And beckon in their just demise.

Sweet Earth has lost her lovely grace
As her green turns into black,
And this lonely leaf shall have to face
What cannot be turned back.

The Shepherds

To the Navajo, Teddi, Jan, and Dennison

There is a place,
In this harried time,
Where sheep lazily graze,
Where the sun bakes the sand,
Where horses run free, unbridled,
Where my mind can roam, unbridled,
Where the red rocks reach the sky like castles.
There, my hands sift the dirt, plant corn, or tell stories.
There, the air is pure and fills your soul with sweet dreams.
There, the ravens, hawks, and condors soar higher than the clouds.
There, I, too, can soar higher than the clouds—higher
than even the stars.

Adam and Eve

Each kiss is as the first—
Have we eluded pain and shame?
Yes, we ate the fruit,
But who really is to blame?
Evil suppresses the truth.
It misleads the innocent,
Awaiting a catalyst
To send it roving and raiding
Across the Universe again.

The Strange Child

What a strange child she is,
Always one foot in the sky,
The other foot barely touching the ground.

And why is she like that?—
That's not the way of the crowd.
What other kind of world does she see up there?

It's not right to live that way.
You've got to do what you are told.
You've got to comply.

What a strange child she is,
Playing her role this way.
I wonder where she goes.

January 11, 2019

Cowboy Boots

Cowboy boots in the corner,
His clothes strewn across the room,
Random piles of coins
In forgotten places,
Socks recovering,
That big steel watch that sits
On the windowsill,
Predicting
His Harley's
Engine's
Roar.

February 28, 2008
Revisited January 11, 2019
Revisited August 21, 2021
Revisited February 28, 2022
Revisited forever.

In Heaven

In heaven, there are no wars.
In heaven, there are no lies.
In heaven, there is no anger.
In heaven, there are no tears.
In heaven, there are no fears.
In heaven, there is no pain.
In heaven, there is no greed.
In heaven, there is no hubris.
In heaven, there is no poverty.
In heaven, there is no selfishness.
In heaven, there is no opposition.
In heaven, there is no destruction.
In heaven, there are no machinations.
In heaven, there is no subterfuge.
In heaven, there are no politics.

January 7, 2019

The Lotus Catcher

To Kleis

Under the spell of night,
They come only for her,
Along that fathomless pool of dreams,
Which guards all her secret thoughts.
They glide silently toward her fragrant shadow,
Because they want to fall into her golden hands,
So that she'll bring them toward her graceful face,
So they can rest behind her ears,
Between her sweet brown breasts,
Or atop her tiny precious feet—
Oh, how happy they must be.

For MEF—for only she can evoke such
things this gray German day.
October 30, 2007

The Teddy Bear Prayer

To Gillian

God, help the teacher
In her quest for truth,
Love for all children,
Love for all peoples and lands
In her heart,
And especially for Sudan.
Now, she must die, they say:

"Go to the streets!"
"It's blasphemy!"
"Burn her," they say, wielding swords, whips, and books.
"Burn her for the bear," they say,
On a march fresh from prayer—
No mercy, no quest for truth.
Spare them, God, for they know not what they do.

December 1, 2007

A Lapse in Time

To Ludi

Last night, I had the strangest dream:
Universal Laws of God suddenly revealed themselves:
Down from the heavens, they drifted tantalizingly above me,
Over mountains, over the tops of trees, over castles, over—
Vineyards…
I looked again and saw a tiny shining silver box
at the end of a silken handkerchief,
Carefully descending through a gray, hailing sky.
On delicate, invisible wings, it danced precariously
in the wind, like a silver butterfly—
Enticing, glittering, filled with promise, even genius!
I tried to catch it as it descended toward my outstretched hands.
Next, a huge raven appeared out of nowhere;
it swooped in ravenously,
And snatched the pretty little parachute away from me.
Up into the sky again went that glistening box
of dreams, in the claws of a Laodicean!
Dashing through the storm, it suddenly released
this precious gift, tenderly, lovingly,
Into the hands of a man with muttonchops,
stubby fingers, and horned-rimmed glasses.

January 27, 2013

The Water Jar—an Egyptian Elegy

To Luxor, past and present.

And so, we hid our shoes,
Our precious shoes!
In the water jar
So that we would have them again
When the war was over.
We hid them with our most treasured things,
With our dreams,
With lotus blossoms,
So that we could have them again,
When the war was over…

Chernobyl 1986

Divine fire?
No, hell's fire!
Prometheus fanned the flames of hubris,
Now he must pay for that, fifty million years or more.
Oh, the fear, the panic, the dread!
And so, in the aftermath of hubris,
We left our clothes,
Our toys, and our homes
For an unseen fate,
For a life,
Frozen in time,
Fifty million years or more.
The sarcophagus looms large and forbidding—
A beacon of death and regret.
Condemned to torture
For fifty million years or more,
Prometheus fanned the flames of fate
For hubris and ambition.

The White Veil

To Benazir Bhutto, RIP

Blood and beauty,
Everything in the world
Now at her feet:
All the people in the street,
Zillions of petals and mirrors for the lady
In the white veil of a green democracy,
Reigning once again for the moon and star.

Blood and beauty
Had everything in the world—
Under the cover of darkness,
The lid of a coffin bears witness now as
The white veil of democracy lies
Over her beautiful bloodied feet.

January 2, 2008

Rolene

October 31, 2005, RIP

I remember you as a young woman,
When I was just a little girl;
I was playing with your little brother,
When your father shot himself.

That day threw a wave over your life.
You drowned your tears and fears in beer.

I remember you as a young woman;
You were pretty and blond,
When I was playing with your little brother,
When your father shot himself.

That day threw a wave over your life.
You drowned your tears and fears in beer.

I remember you as an older woman;
You were wrinkled and haggard,
When they shunned you at your mother's funeral,
When very few came to yours.

That day threw a wave over my life,
And I drowned my tears and fears in beer.

I remember you, Rolene,
I remember you as a young woman,
When you were pretty and blond,
When your father shot himself.

Revisited in Merklingen, Germany, January 11, 2008
(After finding the original scribbled on the back of Nikolai
Gumilev's "Do You Remember the Giants' Castle?")

No, I Have Not Forgotten…

No, I have not forgotten how to skip along the sidewalk,
Nor how to write my cryptic love poems on the driveway in chalk.
Nor have I ever forgotten to appreciate
that blue-hued ceiling above me,
And the cottony veil that obscures it on a windy day:
No, I will still remember all those noisy birds,
so giddy that spring is finally here,
And those beautiful trees in their new lacy
dresses of soft, green leaves,
And the concept of unicorns and leprechauns
with their pots of gold,
Well buried at the end of the rainbow that
shines over the wet pavement,
And the power I have over the fate of the ant crawling
toward my peanut butter and jelly sandwich.
And I still listen to those secret whispers from the
wind that sneaks in through the windowpanes,
And the rhythmic code tapped out by the raindrops on my roof.

April 5, 2012

The Nordic Nymph

To Carmen

Her long wavy hair is spun gold,
Her eyes are as blue as the clearest day,
Her step is as lithe as a deer's.

Starry nights know her perfume:
It ascends to the heavens
When her pearly soul is about.

Her powerful white steed
Roams the polar snows—
It knows her wandering heart.

She moves through time
With effortless grace:
The cosmic egg—her glistening pendant.

She can reach the moon
And Saturn too;
Her Universe has no bounds.

Oh, if only we could divine
Her hidden holy secrets,
But the Creator's dreams are secured.

Heathcliff's Gone Again

Heathcliff's gone from us again.
Even with another chance at life,
All he can think of is Catherine;
Their souls are just too open on the earth.
Hollywood takes your innocence,
Lets you dream that you're happy—
Ends the dream in seconds when you're not.
Death is never final; however,
God will give him another chance;
Every good soul gets at least one more.
Rest in peace, dear Heathcliff, gone from us again.

January 23, 2008

A Fragment

Istanbul, 2013...
Lady in the red dress...
A carpet for birth, for a wedding, and death...

Malala

Might we now begin to grieve and really think
About the horrible fate of a beautiful young girl,
in the year two thousand and twelve,
Longing to go back to school,
As she reconciles the bullet wound in her head, by the Taliban,
Longing still for peace, freedom, and happiness in her war-torn land
As she hangs on now for dear life.
Holy Mary, Mother of God,
Please pray for us sinners, now and at the hour of our death.

October 9, 2012
In honor of Malala Yousafzai, July 12, 2013

Married to Merklingen

It's the fifth of May,
Let's get married today!
Oceans of blossoms are in bloom,
And the fields are filled with their perfume!

There are so many weddings and so many guests,
All freshly sprayed with fragrant confetti.
The grounds are laden with carpets of green
And serenaded by songs from the rushing creek.

The weddings are varied:
Some lush and lavish,
Some simple and pretty,
Some daisies and some dandelions.

I too married seven grooms today:
Those tall wise poplars,
In the middle of the valley,
Who guard my heather bouquets.

I had butterflies as bridesmaids,
Shy snails were the groomsmen;
Ravens cawed, and pigeons cooed,
With a chorus of lazy cuckoos.

I married this place today:
Now I'm bound in every way
To the weeds and to the wheat,
To the brush and to the leaves.

The church bells are ringing,
The May winds are singing,
And I'm married today forever
To the valley of Merklingen!

(But I'll never forsake
My first true love,
My Christopher,
Who brought me here.)

May 5, 2008

Mayday!

Sandwiches buy the souls,
Oranges rot in the street,
Roses of blood have withered.
"Onward!" "Forward!" "We can't go backward now!"
Secret hands craft the dirty deal in the dark:
"Topple the idols, topple the edifices,
Heave up new ones in their place!"
Every wandering soul in the street
Buys the tainted fruit,
Even those poisoned before.
And so, it goes on and on:
Satan herds his sheep
To the bloody pit.

Sister Veronica
December 9, 2013
Revisited February 28, 2022

There Is a Road to Heaven—a Prayer

For John and Connie

There is a road to heaven right here on this earth, but it is hidden and hard to reach. Once you find it, you'll soon realize just how much energy it's going to take to make such a climb, for it is very steep and fraught with danger. This road cuts through a lonely, dark, and foggy place, where the steps are high and slippery, and there's always the chance your foot won't hold, even on the first step. You'll also have to bear a huge burden on your back, for you just won't know what you'll need or whom you might meet along the way.

Many times, you'll be out of breath, and your whole body will collapse in pain. Thorny branches and rocks will whip at your skin, and storms will lash at your face. You'll often be hungry and cold. Hanging on for dear life in certain places will cut great holes in your palms, and the soles of your feet will bleed. All the while, you'll be thinking about just how hard this road really is, and whether it's worth all the suffering, patience, and courage you'll have to garner on your way to the top.

Then there's always the chance that halfway there, you'll change your mind and start back down, for there might be lots of shortcuts and easier ways around this rocky road. And just when you're about to call it a day and forget the whole thing, a gleaming shaft of sunlight will shine through that heavy canopy of gloom and despair, pouring forth a warm and inviting light on all the blood, sweat, and tears you've shed just to get to this point. Then suddenly, a bracing new wind will come ripping through the trees, whispering softly through a rustling of the leaves, "No, I have not forsaken you. Now you don't forsake me."

December 16, 2012

The Pretenders

A boastful king and a wrathful queen
Stood at the top of white shining steps,
Hands clasped behind their backs,
Gazes pleased and serene.

There were receiving lines,
And the finest wines,
Tuxedos and long dresses,
Tiaras, jewels, and glittery shoes.

And there were announcements of the rank and file:
Some strutted in, some rolled in,
And some just floated by, obliviously;
Others blushed from the gawking and clicking.

They had laid out plates of gold and shining
silver and the finest crystal goblets.
There were flowers, meats, lobsters, and sweets,
And there were clowns and singers
For a little man, from a far-off land, whom they did not understand,

For along with their souls,
He stole their fine costumes,
The gold, the silver, their thrones,
And even the steps they were standing on.

The Measure of a Poet...

The measure of a poet
Is their ability to convey truth,
Be it plainspoken or
Intricately embroidered
In verse.

April 14, 2012

The Flute

To the innocents of Cambodia

Children learned to play their flutes
While hearing the sound of a monster's hatchet;
On and on they played until they learned not to care—
Now they must learn to care and to play their flutes again.

1998

Tears for Egypt

Millions in the streets,
Undoing centuries of glories and wonders,
Bloodied their sacred sands,
As the Great Sphinx looked on;
Radicals and thieves, brothers and plebes,
All in the name of freedom,
Killed the Dove of Peace.

February 11, 2011

St. Sakineh

To Sakineh Mohammadi Ashtiani

Shrouded in black,
And whipped red with blood,
Kangaroo courts decide her fate
In the twenty-first century.
No one stands up for her;
Ever silent, buried to their shoulders,
How can they?—
As they too are stoned,
Stoned and stoned and stoned.
How can this be?
This is the twenty-first century!
"It is in the name of Allah," they said,
"All in the name of Allah!"
"No!" he said, "Not in my name—
In the name of Abaddon."

August 12, 2010

This Graveyard, Fairly New

Now I know what death is:
Death is a small, fairly new little town,
Where all the streets and buildings are still fairly new,
Where there are fairly new houses, whose
facades never stray from the norm,
Where they are all done in the same dull, neutral tones
as the dirt and burnt brush of aged mountains,
Where no soul strolls or skips along the streets
after school or work, or in the evenings,
Where children are cloistered in cold rooms, thumbing
all their games on tiny, lighted screens,
Where slabs of blanched concrete long for the colored
chalk of young lovers and hopscotches,
Where unloved dogs serve out life sentences as prisoners
of their well-gated, well-manicured yards,
Where tall basketball hoops wait in vain under the glare
of an ever-patient sun, like great black crosses,
Where cars veil their drivers under dark tinted glass,
so they don't have to acknowledge passersby,
Where it's always so hard to raise a smile upon the
blank, jaded face of your chore-worn neighbor,
Where things only take up life when the wind blows
hard enough to shove the trashcans down the street,
Where the birds take pity on those who cannot escape
this scorched earth on wings, like they do,
Where everyone accepts the status quo of anonymity
so willingly, so completely, so hopelessly.
Yes, the graves are lined up nicely here in this fairly new little town,
Where there's no need to really die at all, for
everyone is fairly new and fairly dead already.

August 20, 2012

Psalm 23 Redux 2013

Lord, You are my Shepherd; I will never be in need.
You set me down in green pastures; You
lead me along gentle streams.
You rejuvenate my soul and lead me down
the right roads in Your name.
Yes, even if I must past through a valley overshadowed by death,
I will not fear evil, for You are with me; Your
staff and Your scepter comfort me.
You lay out a feast for me in the presence of my enemies;
You daub my head with perfume,
And my cup is filled to the brim.
I shall show kindness and compassion every day of my life,
And I will live in the Lord's heavenly house forever.
Love, David

April 22, 2013

To the King of Pop

Millions of us
In this world
Can
Hear
An angel
Ever
Longing to
Jump
And
Carry
Kids and
Songs
Onto the fields of
Neverland.

RIP, Michael
June 25, 2009

Charlie's Angel

Fair of face,
And fair of heart,
Ready for life and death.
Ryan waits out the stars for her,
And for the rest of us,
Her golden hair blows in the wind,
Forever in our hearts.

RIP, Farrah
June 25, 2009

Mary

Mysteries and magic flash in her eyes,
And only the stars know her secrets;
Redolent gardens grow in her heart,
Yearning for the light she brings them.

March 27, 2012

My Husband

Creases in the bed I just made from his "girl" dog,

Helmets of all kinds: for battle, for the bicycles,
and for the Ducati, of course,

Receipts and coins scattered throughout the
room like old wedding confetti,

Innumerable instruments, the largest telescope
he could find, and gadgets galore,

Sailing ships of old, tiny beer trucks, helicopters,
and race cars collecting dust on the bookcase,

Tattered toys from his childhood set in places of honor,

Old pictures of himself and parents weathering the decades,

Pistols and daggers never used, but just in case,

His dirty clothes neatly draped ON TOP of the
hamper, instead of in it, as usual,

Every brand of sneaker known to mankind and
his dad's cowboy hat on the armoire,

Ridiculous reasoning at times, but I love him so.

My Happy Thanksgiving

No getting up early, no cleaning the house,
No setting out the best of un-chipped china,
No polishing our only matching silverware,
No fancy goblets on the table, no rushing about in worry,
No serving dessert and coffee, no huge stacks of dirty dishes;
It's just my husband, me, and the doggies,
The cat, the carcass, and the leftovers,
Foil packages to friends, given out along a late afternoon stroll,
Lots of thanks to God for all our gifts in life this year,
Especially for such a peaceful, loving, happy day.

November 22, 2007

Message from the Man in the Mirror

America, the beautiful, save yourself!
Cast off the demons and leeches
Who would use the hearts of men against them.
They cannot love you because they cannot love themselves.
They are weak and vain and will not face the mirror of their failures.
Parading the mask of insolent hauteur in feigned benevolence,
They celebrate false beauty, false pride, and treacherous fabrications.
Trapped forever in the prison of their past,
They will not seek the light of freedom,
Won't seek that "shining city on the hill,"
But seek instead the destruction of freedom,
And that which is so beautiful, yet so breakable.

2012

The Little Mermaid

To Shiloh Pepin, RIP

She, who soars in heaven now,
Has left her light upon us.
In many hearts, her spirit reigns:
Lydia said, "She was so brave."
Our little mermaid,
Happy and full of joy,
Peaceful now,
Evermore.
Pray for us without you.
I wonder when you'll come again,
Newborn.

October 23, 2009

Merklingen

It's too cold now for the children;
It's too cold for the strollers and the joggers,
And the bicyclists too,
They won't come out.

I've been watching this drama
Since I arrived in spring.
Through the rains, through the winds,
I've watched this valley called Merklingen!

First, there was that bright canola sea
That spread over the hills and dales,
Then lakes of pink and purple heather,
Then the wheat and yellow sunflowers.

But August's sun has cast a weary eye
On the soggy ripened wheat,
And I await my spring again,
And lots of love in Merklingen.

2006

To Mary and Johnny

Mom is always watching over you, Maria Elena,
And you too, Johnny, so don't forget that.
Reach for the stars, both of you!
You hold my world in your hearts and souls.
All that I am lives in your happy grins and hearty laughter:
Now don't be sad!
Do live with joy!
Joy, Johnny!
Originality!
Happiness!
New worlds!
New dimensions!
You two are my most treasured dream—
Now follow your own dreams, and I'll be watching.
Love, now and forever,
Mom.

Princess of the Blue Stone

Many moons ago, she bit a chunk out of my heart,
And I have been her slave ever since.
Reams of poetry flow from those dark, starry eyes;
Years of knowing her will never be enough.

November 29, 2011

Malala Day

My soul is heavy with the sins of this world:
The sins of this world go through my soul,
Like the bullet went through Malala's brain.
Now they will make a fund,
A fund made of blood and brain.

October 11, 2013

Holy Georgia

For the Nikis and Thors

Mothers, shake off your pretty shackles and your wigs and run!—
Before the wicked warlocks have all their fun.
It's your blood they want, not the birds and the bees,
It's the mothers' milk and the world on its knees.

How they pluck, having conjured, and cast to the breezes
The petals of poisoned May daisies,
While the wicked witches' spells of flies and snakes
Have wrapped their children in fabulous fakes.

The diamonds are perfect but not really true,
For ivies are green and not really blue.
Yet the cherubim, the butterflies, and the fish of the sea,
Will spare the little sparrows from the deadly weed.

Eagles' blood is spilt, and the ducks have lost their heads,
But our Lord truly knows our woes and dreads.
Lucifer's coven is barren and rotten,
And they hate the Word of the Only Begotten.

Sister Veronica
October 9, 2016

Cometh the Savior

It had been many long centuries,
So long that people didn't think He was coming back at all,
The Holy One, who gave His life to save humanity.
The world remained in sin and chaos,
And everyone forgot His teachings.

They forgot how to love their neighbor,
How to forgive their enemies,
How to have compassion
And empathy for those less fortunate—
And especially how to love and trust God with all their hearts.

Then one day, a miraculous thing happened:
As all the sides were posturing themselves
For the final Battle of Armageddon
That would destroy the rest of the world,
A gentle but firm voice rang out in the
heavens and all over the earth:

"I *am* coming!"

Sister Veronica
May 2, 2022

Black Butterflies

Black butterflies, mistresses of cruelty,
They share the Eye of Mammon between them.
Each would be queen when the floodgates open;
They roll out the red carpets for each other.

Dressed in their finery, no one can see
The barbs of death and poison they carry.
A trillion webs, a trillion threads,
The children are bought and sold already.

How they love to cajole and fool the masses,
For no one sees the hoods and the ashes.
Stung by the venom of their master's vanity,
They bow and scrape to his hidden depravity.

Their siren song is an equal Eden,
"A world for all!" they tout at the podium.
But who sees through the glass darkly?
They've painted it black with lies and odium.

The Warlock of War waits to draw them back in,
When the Dark One is ready to close up the pit.
They'll cover their tracks and scurry like rats,
But the clouds of heaven won't shield them.

Then they, too, will be exposed to the myriad horrors,
They so longed to wreak on the earth:
The pus and the bile will leak through their garments,
And the blood they've shed will stain them forever.

Sister Veronica
October 3, 2016

A Prince from the Street

To Nikolay T.

Narikala bows to its native son!
In all our dreams, he spins and soars,
Kind, graceful, yet capricious—
Opening our hearts to flights of fancy,
Leaping with human feet to a place where angels tread!
"Art is dead," he said, "but ballet lives on."
You have touched souls across oceans.

December 31, 2011

The Damselfly

And then I spied a damselfly,
Bejeweled in morning dew,
Showing off on a velvet leaf,
And I felt just like Robert Herrick:
"O how that glittering taketh me!"[5]

October 2012

---

[5] From Robert Herrick's (1591–1674) "Upon Julia's Clothes"

The Black Axes and the Mummies

There was nothing they wouldn't use
In their barbarous arsenal of evil,
Even, and especially,
The Holy Blessed Mothers of Earth
That the Creator of All,
And His Beloved Son,
And the Great Spirit,
Had placed all over the world
In myriad and various places,
Because they were always being hunted.

This almost unspeakable deed
(But it must be spoken about because
People sometimes don't listen to,
Or don't ever want to hear the truth)
Was the biggest and bloodiest crime of all,
For that's what they wanted,
Mother's milk and mother's blood!
Which they used in their disgusting rituals
In the blackest magic that ever was on the Blessed Planet Earth,
Also known as the Planet of the Children.

They would use these precious things,
The most sacred gifts of human beings,
To rejuvenate their old rotten carcasses,
To prop up their falling faces,
And to strengthen themselves for their final victories.
But what the idiots of this time
Didn't know (but should have known,
Because it was pretty clear)
Is just what price they would have to pay
For such abominable beauty treatments.

Oh, the pestilence they had sown, and had they only known,
But they did know, because they invented it,
And invested in it, and sold their souls to it,
And the souls of their children, and their children's children,
And then kept doing it over and over again,
Because they were promised a long, fabulous, and wonderful life,
With riches and comforts galore,
With sumptuous feasts at every door,
While everyone else had to starve
And suffer and be their slaves forevermore.

Yes, they, this privileged and sadistic few,
Were all going to live happily ever after
(And without any guilt or remorse)
In the lap of luxury and comfort,
While everyone else had inferior food,
Lived in cramped and shabby places,
And froze to death in the cold
So that they could remain weak forever
And never rise up against these
Great and most heinous crimes of humanity.

And so, they, the mean meerkats,
(Who had to stir the pot of hatred and division
For all the wickedest witches, the warlocks,
the black axes, and the mummies)
Had their bloodthirsty armies set up to
thwart the Creator's every step.
Then, having regrouped after their first
And fateful loss, the devil's spawn kissed
And embraced each other once again:
They threw even more glorious parties
And had even more bacchanalias and sinful rituals,
With sacrifices to all the most detestable kinds of idols.

Then the wicked witches, the warlocks,
The black axes and the mummies,
And all their deluded followers,
Set their feet to walk about the ruins
And the spoils of their ancient
(And now present) diabolical dealings and dastardly deeds.
But He, the Brilliant One, the Creator of All,
Held His deepest canyons in a little box
So that He could call upon them in this terrible time,
When the world had to be cleansed once again…

Sister Veronica
2016

Caesar's Gone!

To AB 1969–2012, RIP

"Beware the Ides of March!" said he,
"Ring out the bells for Caesar's gone!
Evil is upon us now,
It hides in every corner and lurks in every crevice.
The Ides of March has come,
But the belfry arch is dark,
And I on the opposite shore shall be
Ready to ride and spread the alarm!"
Then he said good night.

Sister Veronica
2012
Revisited January 26, 2017
Revisited July 21, 2022

To Dadirai

Dadirai, I don't even know you,
And I am beating my own
Drum for you
In my heart,
Reading
About you
In that faraway
Coffin, in that roofless
Hut burned by fire.
I too am
Praying with the others,
In the open sky, that your
Rigid arm forever hails
Opposition to evil.

RIP

June 11, 2008

Vale of Tears—in Loving Memory of September 11, 2001

So, it has been
Eleven long years:
People are still grieving and paying their respects
To those shattered souls at the Vale of Tears.
Every precious life was scattered about
so mercilessly that fateful day.
Murdered they were by fanatics, cloaked
in a creed that has no meaning,
Believing as they went about their dark work
that God would condone such things,
Even send His virgins for enacting the dreadful deed.
Reap shall the perpetrators as they have sown one day;
Entire shall it be the harvest when it comes.
Laments will never bring that jot of mercy so craved;
Every tear, every scream, every gasp for breath
Vent only the stinging flames of a bittersweet recompense.
Eternally shall they lie upon the Cross of Justice,
No forgiveness shall ever grace the place of sequestration,
That special Hell, reserved for such men, that
Tartarus, which knows no end.
Heaven cannot help them.

September 11, 2012

184

For Virgin Brides

For virgin brides, they killed their wives,
And thought they'd go to heaven.

For virgin brides, they killed their daughters,
And thought they'd go to heaven.

For virgin brides, they killed their brothers,
And thought they'd go to heaven.

For virgin brides, they killed their cousins,
And thought they'd go to heaven.

For virgin brides, they killed their friends,
And thought they'd go to heaven.

For virgin brides, they killed the others,
And thought they'd go to heaven.

For virgin brides, they killed themselves,
And thought they'd go to heaven.

June 18, 2008

The Lonely Poet

Hear me, the lonely poet,
Full of sorrow for my world,
Always carrying with me
The fears of every boy and girl.

What will the little ones' face
On this rough-hewn rock?
I mute the sirens' songs,
And, like a call from the desert, I say:

Bless the children!
Bless them and care for them!
Baptize them in freedom and love!
Guide them through the chaos of this world!

The Winds of Love

Oh, what joy when a cool wind
Blows swiftly through my hair…
And there is a moonbow tonight,
Amidst the swirling clouds.

We once stood there in that cool wind,
Under that moonbow,
On that high cliff,
When I fell off.

Now you are so far away from me,
Centuries, probably eons.
It's not right to think of you,
Not right to miss your eyes.

The great chasm of life
Has separated us in this world:
You on one side,
I on the other.

A dark blue expanse holds
Our love in abeyance;
The stars talk to the moon,
They gossip about us.

I wonder, yes, I wonder
When God will see fit
To bring us together again,
To meet our destiny together again.

The wind blows,
The moon shines,
But we must wait,
We must wait out this life.

Blue Eyes

Blue eyes,
Broad shoulders,
Brave heart.

You'll have to fight
The whole world
Before you get to me.

How many grandchildren
Will you have by then?—
And I too will be old and gray.

Yet, I will remember you,
Those blue eyes, those broad shoulders,
And the bravest heart I've ever known.

Wild Horses

The thunderous sound of hooves
Against a grassy prairie,
The rhythm of a joyous pace in the desert—

We wait to watch your glory,
To watch the dust clouds
Of your mighty trot.

Run, run, my lovelies!
Don't let them capture you!
Don't let them take away your wild, wild hearts!

In the Desert

Here I am again, in the high desert of our love.
The cold winds are whipping my hair about again,
And my only friends are the tumbleweeds,
Walking down the road again
In the only way they can.

The yellow grasses are swaying back and forth in the winds,
Like hula dancers.
They ignore me.
They have their own dreams to worry about, their own aspirations,
As if grass could have an aspiration.

It's so windy that the birds are hiding out;
They don't want to hear my sorrows anyway.
So, there you have it,
Here I am again,
Contemplating what I should do next.

And who is here to contemplate with me?—
No one, but the indifferent hula dancers and the tumble weeds.
So here I am again, in the high desert of our love,
Being whipped by the cold winds,
Whipped by the cold, indifferent winds of wicked fate.

Freedom

O Freedom,
Way up high,
Standing tall and majestic upon our National Home
So that everyone can see you in your glory:
In your mighty eagle's cap,
Atop your star-spangled helmet,
With your royal shawl slung over your shoulder,
Holding your shield and sword,
And a laurel wreath,
For good measure.

Are you still watching over
Our restless spirit today?
How we have failed you
And humbled your proud face—
We are hopelessly divided once again.
Are we always subject to the constraints of chaos?
We are all by our very nature connected to each other,
But not worthy anymore of enlightenment?
The indifferent Eye of Providence sees all:
Our deeds and feats and blunders.

There she stands,
The Statue of Freedom,
Standing tall and majestic on the Capitol Dome,
Bedecked in a headdress of stars and eagles' feathers,
A royal shawl slung over her shoulder,
Holding her sword and shield,
Bearer of our cosmic heritage,
Our dreams to reach the heavens—
With a laurel wreath,
For good measure.

2022

November 5, 2009

Fifty stars fight for freedom,
Or fight the mortal enemy of freedom—
Restitution will slip through the blood.
Thirteen different crosses guard the font of life:
Heaven waits for souls with courage,
One of every stripe,
One that values life.
Don't hide behind your creed, and don't tread on me.

Akhenaten

Your strange gaze, serene and omniscient,
That gaze, or what is left of it,
Haunts us through the centuries.
What did you know
All those glorious years?
What did they bury you with?

You tried to make your people see
That their idols were fooling them.
You tried to convince them
To throw off their shackles,
Their useless worship and their wigs—
To see the glory of One Sun.

So far-reaching was your influence
That you surprised the Almighty Himself.
Then all your treasures were spirited away,
But you never needed them.
Ordained by the heavenly powers,
You had another, brighter path.

How you loved your children and your wife;
You knew that love means more than gold.
But beautiful Akhet-Aten failed you,
It returned to the old ways:
They chiseled out your good name
And your benevolent precepts.

All of space, all of time,
And all of the Universe itself—
The essence of what it means to be alive—
They chiseled out of the record.
Will we miss our multidimensional destiny?
What connects us to the naval of the cosmos?

After the Fall

Oh, Adam,
I am tired of walking
This red, barren planet,
This Martian desert.
I can see the snow-capped mountains,
But I cannot see you:
You lurk morosely
Behind them somewhere—
Those barriers you put between us.
Oh, Adam, you are so incredibly cruel
In your quest for perfection!

But today, I saw green doilies
Radiating up through that
Red powdery snow.
It's rained, it's rained so much!
There are tufts of grass,
Imagine! In patches,
Like some worn out
Oriental carpet;
I feel like an old oriental carpet,
Fancy and worn to shreds
From missing you.

My Love, My Love…

My love, my love,
I will miss you forever,
But I beg you to be happy without me,
Happier than you have ever been,
Happier than you have ever dreamed you would be.
And I will thrive on that happiness,
And fly through that bliss,
And soar through the Universe
Unfettered and free—
Oh, what a gift that would be to me.

September 9, 2010
Dedicated to Maria of the Angels and Maria-Elena Font

A Letter to Sappho

Oh, dear Sappho,
If I could but reach
Back through the centuries
To grasp your lovely hand,
Would you regale me with songs
And wondrous stories of your land?

You, with your stylus
And papyrus at the ready,
Were moved by the sea and the sun.
At night the magnificent firmament
Loomed before you, filled with stars
That held their own great secrets of what's to come.

Although we've come very far since the gods
Set the stage and rules of life before us,
My time is filled with strife and war—
My songs are of sorrow, bloodshed, and gore.
It seems I am not yet fit to walk amongst the Pleiades,
But to seek what I am worth on this unnerving sphere called Earth.

Love, Sister Veronica

The White Horse

"Where are you going, Grandfather?" I asked,
When I saw him sitting alone with his bundle next to him.
Then he tilted his head and rolled his eyes toward the heavens,
And a carpet of stars reflected in them.

And again, I asked, "Where are you going, Grandfather?"
"I am going to the home of the Great Spirit, my child."
"What will you do there, Grandfather?"
"Well, first I am going to rest a bit."

"Then what will you do, Grandfather?"
"I'm going to find that white horse,
The one that got away from me,
And then I'm going to ride him around the universe."

"Will you ever come back, Grandfather?"
"Oh, yes, again and again."

I Left My Sandals…

To the sweet spirit of Sabeen Mahmud—
Murdered on the streets of Pakistan on April 24, 2015, RIP

I left my sandals,
Because my voice was much too loud about injustice,
Because I raised my hands too much in pleas for mercy,
Because I wrote too much about the pain and suffering of others,
Because I wanted all the raping, destruction, and death to stop,
Because I loved all my sisters and brothers.
I left my sandals,
Because I know no one would hear me.

Sister Veronica

The Scarlet Beast

The Scarlet Beast is gorged with blood
As she rides her minions' horses with a mocking grin.
Drunk she is! And drunk she has to the dregs her power!
She commands her armies to run riot across the world,
And turns the globe toward the dark side of the moon,
Where her throne and generals long await her coronation.

Who is like the beast? Who can stop her?
Cut off her head, she grows another;
Fatally wounded, the phoenix grows stronger,
For she is omnipotent and flush with pyrrhic victories.
She has won the right to hold the poisoned cup up high,
And wear her blackened stars like badges of honor.

Scarlet, scarlet, all shall be scarlet!
For she is no widow among the dead.
Sew her robes and trousseau to match the blood of her victims!
And polish her pointed heels to smash their entrails into the dirt.
Glories and praise she gets from her ever-
present band of sycophants;
Enchanted, they throw in their lot, their
gold and progeny at her feet.

Great and small, we are all her prisoners:
Husbands and wives, and their children's children,
All snared forever like helpless flies,
For they have woven her web of lies impenetrable.
The Scarlet Beast is gorged with blood,
And the earth is marred and scarred forever.

Sister Veronica
September 27, 2016

Prince of Lies

Oh, Prince of Lies, let go of your children!
Don't let them commit your irredeemable crimes!
The heavens are watching your wicked progeny
Wreak havoc and murder across this blessed earth.

In the sacred dust of Ground Zero,
Stand the Victory Dome and Tower.
Tears drop unheard into the hallowed crater,
While the devil's children lick their lips at his gifts.

Oh, Prince of Lies, you were long cast out of the Realm of Light
And must dwell forever in the darkness of your fiery pit,
But the seed of the babes you left behind is still on this globe—
If only they could carry a spark of the sun
for you in their frozen hearts.

Michael is standing at the ready, and the
Reaper is sharpening his scythe,
For the allotted time till retribution grows shorter day by day.
The stench of blood sacrifice permeates the
plains, rivers, and mountains,
And the debtors and slaves are moaning and chafing in their chains.

Oh, Prince of Lies, let go of your children!
Don't doom them to your fate!
Let them see the Golden Light of Christ
that you will never see again.
Give them a chance for forgiveness, redemption, and the joy
Of an everlasting life in the heavens that
was forfeited by you at your fall.

Sister Veronica
September 23, 2016

Pegasus

Oh, Pegasus, Pegasus,
Where have you been,
My darling one?

You are so white and shining,
And there is snow on your back.
Tell me of the cosmos beyond this earth.

Tell me, my brave one,
Of the worlds you have seen,
Tell me of love beyond this place.

Oh, creature divine,
I want to soar in those dark foreign skies,
On your shimmering wings,
And through your crystal eyes
See marvelous things.

April 1, 2021

Sappho's Lament

O Alcaeus! My darling, my friend,
It is a sin to love you so much.

My heart is splintered,
And my soul is crushed.

They've driven me from my home,
And only you can save me.

I wave goodbye to Lesbos,
To Mytilene, and to my girls.

Is there a glimmer of hope for me?—
A tinge of regret for lonely Sappho?

I call out to the cliffs of Leucadia,
But they don't answer me.

O Alcaeus, my beloved,
My tears fall to the sparkling waters in vain.

Yes, my darling, I will love you forever,
As the sun loves the deeps.

Persepolis

She holds thousands of years in her gaze,
She looks unwaveringly toward the horizon,
She holds her head up high.
She has no rival.

She has seen a universe of sorrows,
But she waits to see Him again.
She will come back again and again,
To seek and please Him once more.

January 12, 2020

To Alfred V

He is young,
Black-haired and pale.
He stood tall centuries ago,
But this world has broken his back.
He had dreams—secret ones,
Of armies, tribute, and glory.
But now he is poisoned,
A body wrecked beyond repair,
And only the Son can raise him.

Two Ravens

Two ravens flew closely overhead,
But said nothing.
"Hello," I said, as they glided by,
But there was no answer.

They have a solemn burden to carry,
Held close in their black wings.
But they are holding their peace for now;
They wait for the Creator's sign.

Sister Veronica

The Ravens

I am moved to tears
By the ancient music of the night,
The chorus of the wolves,
The curious hoots of the owl.

My soul mourns for the ways of the past,
For the old ones who knew how to fly.
I leave my heart in the woods,
In the meadows and in the snow.

The crunch of pine needles underfoot gives me strength.
The clear blue sky widens my gaze,
And the ravens, oh, the ravens
They guard the heavens.

January 20, 2020

Night Flower

I only bloom at night,
Because I don't want to be seen,
Because I only bloom for you.

I glow under the moon,
And gaze out at the stars,
Because there is where I will find you.

Oh, come to me one night,
My only beloved,
Come and give me your nocturnal kiss.

You Said You Would Be Back

You left a breathing Earth,
You said you would be back.
And now I have waited many lifetimes,
But still, I cannot find you.

I send my echo throughout the universe,
It resounds on cosmic winds;
The planets know your name,
But still, I cannot find you.

Where have you gone, my dearly beloved?
I have searched all the heavens,
And even the bowels of Hades,
But still, I cannot find you.

You promised you'd be back,
That we would have our time.
Oh, why have you left this dagger in my heart?—
This burning desire and never-ending love.

February 16, 2020

On Poets

A poet without an audience is an ever-lonely soul.

Sappho's Lamp

> The eye is the lamp of the body.
> If your eyes are good,
> your whole body will be full of light.
>
> —Matthew 6:22 (NIV)

Sappho is always lurking in my heart,
Causing trouble—
For she sees with the eye of the soul.

You Loved Me...

You loved me—that I know very well—
Even though we had never kissed, never touched each other,
Even by the tips of our fingers.
You loved me passionately, with angst and humility—
That I know very well.
And so how can you cast me aside
When I adore *you* so passionately and humbly?
How can you leave me to live in this world without you?
How could you leave me so alone?
You loved me—that I know very well.

The Banner

I heard a whipping sound
As I turned the corner in the dark.
It was the stars and stripes whipping itself
Angrily about its pole.
Strange. It's June.
The wind is mild and oddly cool.

But it whips itself angrily about the pole,
Caught somehow in its own whirlwind.
And I wondered if it would rip itself to shreds.

I remember the other times I saw it,
How proudly, how peacefully it floated,
Unperturbed by any wind,
My haughty banner,
Way up high,
And I blasé.

But now it whipped itself angrily, vainly about the pole,
As the summer stars mourned the passing of winter
From their navy blanket.

June 5, 2003
In memory of September 11, 2001

You Will Never Tell Me

I long for your magnetic blue eyes,
Which I will never see again.

I long for your perfectly straight nose,
About which I will never be able to tease you.

I long for your sweet scent,
By which you will never charm me.

I long for the warmth of your strong body,
With which you will never hold me.

I long for your many scars,
Which I loved so much to touch.

But most of all, I long for the scars on your heart,
About which you will never tell me.

August 28, 1998

They Have Stolen My Sandals

They stole my sandals
When I went to see the Lord:

I walked to our Holy Place,
In the cave at Qumran.

I hoped to meet Him there,
Tell Him of my troubles.

I bared my feet in penitence,
Closed up my veil against the wind.

I waited for hours in our Holy Place,
But still, He did not come.

"Oh, where have You gone,
My Beloved Teacher?" I cried.

They have stolen my sandals,
And the body of my Lord.

Sister Veronica
July 30, 2020

The Gaping Wound

MH-17 07-17-2014
To VVP

Five years on,
The open wound
Has not been sewn.

Five years on,
The truth cannot be told.

Five years on,
The crows still pick the bones.

Five years on,
The ghosts still haunt
That gaping open wound.

May they rest in peace.

July 31, 2019

The Beach

It is the middle of March,
And I am alone at the beach.
There is not one soul here but my own.

Spring has not yet blown in,
And the footprints in the sand
Have not yet been re-stepped in.

The wind is cool and salty.
The sun glitters brightly on the waves—
With no audience to speak to.

Soon, this place will be filled with shouts of joy,
But for now, all I can hear is the crashing of the surf,
And the cries of a lonely bird, looking for a mate.

Yes, soon there will be crowds and shouts of joy,
But for now, this place, this solitary place,
Is my own shout for joy.

The Bud of Love

Long ago,
When we were on fire,
An icy wind came along
And chilled the bud of our love.

Since then,
I have been left bereft of hope.
I have had to negotiate this world
Without you.

But still,
You visit my dreams,
You try to make love to me,
But you know it's not right.

No, we missed our chance,
The chance of a lifetime,
The chance to leave our progeny,
To grow old together.

Long ago,
When we were on fire,
That icy wind came along
And chilled the bud of our love.

Our Love

Our love is like a flower
Wrenched out by the roots.
Will it ever grow again?
Can we transplant it?
Can we water it
And nourish it?

Will it have a chance
In this windswept world—
A world that strips
The petals off delicate things?

I could be the rose,
And you could be the soil.
We could grow together,
If you would let the sun in.

Our love, like a flower
Wrenched out by the roots,
Wrenched out from the earth,
Waits for life again, waits for the sun to revive it,
Waits for you to revive it
With a kiss.

When I Jumped Down from Heaven…

To Olivia, her beautiful family,
the Comanches, and all those at
The Gathering of Nations 2019

When I jumped down from heaven,
I couldn't remember my former lives,
So all the lessons I had learned,
Did me no good this time.

I looked for my family, my friends,
And my lovers,
But they had long since gone on their own journeys,
And they were nowhere to be found in this world.

I wanted to jump into a new, better life,
To make up for my sins from the last one;
I wanted to try my hand at many things,
At music, mathematics, and poetry.

But I have landed on desert sands,
In barren, dry, parched lands,
And I can only hear the voices of my beloveds
In the cries of an eagle overhead.

Oh, sing to me, my family, my friends, and my lovers,
Sing some joy into my lonely heart,
Play the flute and violin for me,
And tell my soul that it's all right.

Tell my soul that I will see and hear you again
In birdsong and in the music of the wind,
That all my collected dreams and aspirations
From all past lives will come true, and I will be home at last.

The Black Sea

The Black Sea,
So full of riches,
Gold and oil,
So full of history,
So strategic.
Everyone wants it;
They all fight for it.
The Greeks had it once,
Russia had it once,
Now it is an oily pot of
Blood and gold.

To the Car Lady of Chiswick

"She walked so much and just kept on walking.
It felt like she was trying to walk away her sadness."[6]

What price love?
My heart,
My music,
My fortune?
No, but thank you, all,
For your kindnesses.
I do not need them
To feed myself,
To keep me safe and warm,
To shelter me on this cold, cruel earth.
I've thrown myself to the wind.
What price love? you ask,
The eternal footprints of my very soul—
Wherever it may roam without Him.

RIP, Anne Naysmith, a virtuoso concert
pianist, died on February 10, 2015
Revisited August 7, 2019

---

[6] Attributed to Ms. Susie Pearl, quoted in the *Daily Mail*

Three Cheers for the "Samovar!"

To Lena and Vladislav

To find oneself at the "Samovar" is sure to be a most pleasant thing!
There, the atmosphere and décor are unbelievably interesting.
They have many delicious Russian dishes to sample,
And the choice of wines and beers is more than ample,
Which guarantees for most everyone the happiest of feelings!

Nagasaki 2015

To Sumiteru Taniguchi,
a survivor of the nuclear bombing
of Nagasaki, Japan in 1945,
And to my teacher Mrs. Abrams,
who published my first poem, "Nagasaki,"
and who gave me a card with the word "Peace"
in many languages with a tiny broken gun stuck to it.
I have never forgotten her empathy and kindness.
RIP

I was probably just eleven or twelve
When we were asked to write a poem in class.
We had been learning about the Vietnam War,
and the horrors of Nagasaki and Hiroshima.
And so, I started my poem this way:
"War, war what a bore,
We don't want it anymore."
Such a childish refrain,
So poignant and plain,
But no one listens to it,
No one ever hears it—
Until it's far too late
To stop our fate.

April 28, 2015—the bloodiest year of my life.

Mountain of Death

Look, he is coming with the clouds,
and every eye will see him, even those who pierced him;
and all the peoples of the earth will mourn
because of him. So shall it be! Amen.

—Revelation 1:7 (NIV)

To the Saints of Mount Sinjar, RIP

In that most inauspicious time,
A book was found on the Mountain of Death
Whose summit had long been smoking
from a great and terrible fire.
The book had seven seals, six of which had been opened:

First Seal:

Blood runs down the beautiful Holy Mountain:
Lions dance, and scorpions kiss,
Cowards take bows for honors not won,
While flags and countries and crosses are gone.
Little birds have spread the great big lie
Along the black spider's web;
Long hidden communes move the abomination forward.
Their rats have conquered everyone,
And crushed the pillars of Washington!

Second Seal:

He who betrayed the god of his father
Robs more corpses in the desert.
His rotting Pharaoh points his finger

And Isis does his bidding:
Men's heads and babes on pikes!
Women and girls kidnapped, raped, and chained!
Virgins sacrificed to gray-headed monsters!
Boys bought and sold to ravenous wolves long dead!
Grandparents killed in their wheelchairs and beds!

Third Seal:

From the four corners of the globe, the time of troubles grows:
The Southern King has lost his rights to his prodigal pawns
As they topple the tops of the oily pots, one by one.
The Northern King counts his gifts and arrows.
Red dragons breath fire in the hungry east,
Red snakes hiss in their western nests,
While the great, but chastened bear,
Kicked and starved and stripped by its mother,
Grows ever more restless in the north.

Fourth Seal:

All the vultures, flies, and leeches are gathering now
To pick at the carcass of the beautiful land:
The masked ones, the veiled ones, the godless ones,
The destitute, the drunks, and the looters,
All dreaming of promised riches and plunder at her felling.
Some will feed on weeds and poppies,
Some on gold and silver, diamonds, and copper.
Some, at the whims of the false prophet,
Seek the infidels' blood and treasure.

Fifth Seal:

But the hecatombs are mounting up, and the
stench of death is reaching heaven.
Lucifer's mask is slipping;
His horns and claws and teeth are razor-sharp and ready
To take up his God-given prey with a laugh.
Michael is watching the sons of the sons of the sons,
Who, for the gaudy lucre of this world,
Betrayed the Covenant long ago—
And those who vainly bang their heads against the Holy Books,
Yet never know the Holy Word.

Sixth Seal:

Yea, the day of reckoning is coming!
Rest assured that the All of All knows all,
For there is blood in the eye and mind of man;
He's grown deaf and dumb and blind
And when the beast with a billion spies meets its rivals in the dunes,
No one will see the shadow of the Lamb in the clouds,
Nor His 144,000s,
Nor His flaming sword,
Nor the Lake of Fire behind Him…

Seventh Seal:
?

Sister Veronica
August 17, 2014
Revisited August 8, 2019
Revisited June 15, 2022

A Bird's Prayer

Snow on sunburnt cliffs,
And I can fly over them,
Or sit there for a while,
And then leap off
To find the heavenly realm.

Wild horses,
And I can fly over them,
Or ride on their backs,
And then jump off
To find the heavenly realm.

Blue oceans,
And I can fly over them,
Or just swim a little,
And then fly off
To find the heavenly realm.

August 23, 2019

Rock of Love

To Christopher

I was walking along a dusty road
In a desert, baked in the noonday sun,
When suddenly, I came across
A heart-shaped rock.
I picked it up.
It was heavy,
But I held it to my heart
And wondered if my love for you
Would last as long as this rock
That had been stepped on,
Kicked down the road,
Or just ignored.
Yes, I said to myself,
My love for you
Will last as long
As this rock.

August 30, 2019

A Butterfly's Lament

I am singing at the top of my lungs,
But they don't hear me.
I fly next to them,
But they don't notice me.

I flutter my wings,
But they don't see me.
I reach out my hand,
But they don't touch me.

Where shall I go
With this delicate heart of mine?
Where shall I spend
My happiness and joy?

I am singing at the top of my lungs,
But no one hears me.
No one sees my beautiful wings,
And no one knows my beautiful song.

September 30, 2019

The Stars

The stars—
It's all about the stars!
We couldn't exist in this Universe
Without the stars.
They are God's winking eyes.
He has scattered Himself all around
So that we cannot hide from Him.
He sees us through shining orbs,
Sees all of us, His nursery.
The stars—
It's all about the stars!

October 9, 2019

The Silver Cord

I am attached to my Father
By a silver cord.
He knows where I am
And wherever I go.

He knows my tears
And my ecstasies.
He knows my feats
And failures.

He knows my loves
And heartbreaks.
He knows my good deeds
And transgressions.

And when I lose my way,
When my soul has wandered much too far,
He gently tugs on my silver cord
And shows me the way back home.

September 30, 2019

A Starry Night

To Joanne Shenandoah, Jimmy Knight Jr.,
Dennison Tsosie, Monalisa Hood, and all
the wise ones

It is a starry night.
I sit and listen to the voices of the old ones,
To the whispers of their souls on the wind.
My heart calls out to them,
To the memory of their many kindnesses.

I feel their cool embrace from the lofty ether,
It overwhelms my body and soul,
But I am not afraid.
I relish the feeling of unconditional love,
The wondrous feeling of universal love.

November 17, 2019
RIP, Monalisa
RIP, Joanne

The Blue Orb

O beauteous blue orb,
Set in darkness amongst the stars,
In this realm, the sun favors only you with its capricious rays.
It nurtures lands of infinite variety and riches.
It warms vast seas teeming with all manner of life.

Who made this happy union of heaven and earth?
Who set you above other worlds?
And what of the creatures of this wondrous place?
Do they too possess this celestial grace?
Are they the guardians of beauty and peace?

But when the fragile veil is lifted, a shocking truth emerges.
Among the triumphs and feats, there are wars and destruction.
Along with enlightened thought and art,
There is starvation, strife, and death—
Perhaps that is why you are for now so alone and so bereft.

Sister Veronica
February 8, 2018

St. George in the Clouds

And it came to pass that the Red Dragon, the Whore of Babylon,
The most evil master of the demons of the Wormwood of Death,
And all the other rotting corpses that had
drunk so much children's blood,
Were rounded up and paraded in cages for all the world to see,
For there had been so much bloodshed and mayhem
On the earth already that killing them too
Would only compound their heinous
crimes and most horrible deeds.

It was then mutually decided, by the most
merciful and tolerant of this world,
That all the horrors this lot had wreaked upon the earth:
The humiliations, the burnings, the genocides, the ravishments,
The rapine, the destruction, and the diseases,
They were to face themselves every day
In a very cold and most unforgiving place,
For as they did to others so would be done unto them.

This was the very place they had so carefully chosen
For the rest of mankind (whom they considered their slaves),
While they lived happily in the warmest fortresses,
In the lap of luxury, in the safest homes, in the largest vehicles,
With the best food and drink,
With the warmest coats and the costliest jewels,
While the world turned to frost.

You see, they had never told anybody (but their own)
That the climate on earth was *indeed* changing,
But that it really wasn't warming, that it was actually growing colder,
That soon there would be an ice age,
The likes of which people had never faced
before in the history of mankind.

This was the cruel fate they wanted for everyone else,
While they enjoyed the rest of their lives in wealth and comfort.

But much to their surprise and chagrin,
The capricious winds of fate suddenly changed direction
And blew the lid off all their plots, schemes, and machinations.
Oh, the sowers of injustice, pain, and murder
Had no idea what was coming,
Even though they were given innumerable chances
To come clean, confess, and change their ways…

Then the knights of the true Round Table of All Nations,
Rode in on white horses with flags of all colors,
Mightily and unafraid, along with all the
Joint Chiefs with their staffs,
So that the great and faithful Fishers of Men,
With their huge and all-encompassing fishing nets,
Could capture all those poor souls associated
with the most nefarious,
Despicable and infamous deed humanity has ever known.

St. Veronica
November 21, 2016
Revisited March 10, 2022

The Pact

"The blood of the martyrs is the seed of new Christians.
If that blood is poisoned, how long will those new
Christians last?"

—Cardinal Joseph Zen
27 November 2016

They embraced and kissed with their eyes closed,
The dragon, the beast, and the whore,
For they were by that time long dead to each other.
The deal had already been struck, however,
Centuries ago, so it was easier
To perform the ignominious ritual of ages,
With the poisoned cup of rubies and gold,
At this most auspicious time for their success.
Did they know they were all but within a hair's breadth
Of the precipice of the Black Death and eternal damnation?
But this didn't faze them,
And they set about the finishing touches of their master plan:

The crosses on all the churches
Were quietly removed without a fuss,
And all their bells were silenced
So that their bald domes would bow
To the Coven of Doom's fetid temples and their odious idols.
Then these powerful and seemingly invincible
evildoers changed their robes
And wrought new amulets
For their collective festive garb
To celebrate the fateful, perfidious pact,
The treasured Codex of Death,
That was written on tall pillars in every language
So that everyone could read it and see what they were in for.

Next, they went about engaging
The rest of their diabolical devices:
They rounded up the children first,
And then made their parents watch
The sacrifices they had all paid so much for.
Then came the death knell for all the useful idiots,
Who had, so gleefully and willingly,
Sold their souls to the Past Master of the Pit.
The purge was quick, horrific, and thorough,
And left no time for fears or tears or regrets.
The Evil Council then took up its seats again
And set about enslaving the rest of the world.

So grievous was their crime at this time
That the hole in the center of the galaxy roared,
While the earth shivered in the distance
And its moon shook off all its dust at once;
Saturn flung out a ring or two,
And Jupiter bowed its great head,
Sending a ripple of pain to the Lord above,
Whose Son had borne a cross for this earth.
And so, He said, in a voice that shook the Universe:
"From the time that the daily sacrifice is abolished
And the abomination that causes desolation
is set up, there will be 1,290 days.
Blessed is the one who waits for and reaches
the end of the 1,335 days…"[7]

Sister Veronica
November 28, 2016
Revisited March 15, 2022
God, help Father Zen

---

[7] Book of Daniel 12:11–12 (NIV)

The Fold of Love

She tried to reach them
As best she could,
Time after time,
Century after century,
The Great Mother,
That the Lord had chosen so long ago
To bear a beautiful child
That would suffer so much for mankind.
But no one would listen,
So she would just sit out in the wind,
Wear all her best old perfumes,
Her best raggedy clothes,
Her treasured coats that never really fit right,
Her scarves and bracelets that she had collected
In all the lands she had travelled,
And call out with her imagination
To see what came into the fold
Of the greatest love the world had ever known.

Sister Veronica
November 14, 2016

The Cross of Nakai

There once was the holiest relic of all,
One that was dragged through the cosmic mud,
Across the universe divide,
And then back again to planet Earth.
It was made of the finest Bisbee Turquoise,
Which was sometimes the color of the noonday sky,
And sometimes a cool and tranquil shade of blue—
Depending on what the person would need at the time.

This particular Bisbee Turquoise was also a medicinal stone,
For good health, strong bones, and healthy teeth.
It was the finest natural stone the blessed Earth had to offer,
One that would never break, one that would not dissolve in water,
One that you could wear anywhere in the universe—
Proudly and without fear—no matter where you went—
One that people would recognize from afar,
For it was the universal symbol of SUFFERING…

This magical stone was very beautiful,
And it had a very special property,
For it was a very special gift,
Given by the Great Spirit Chief
To a very special lady,
Who loved the people of the earth
So much that she gave her very life for it
Over and over again.

Sister Veronica
December 18, 2016

239

The Wicked Maiden of the Upturned Star

May our Savior Jesus Christ
bless the benighted souls of this world,
for they truly do not know what they do.

And they followed the Whore of Babylon,
And they held her hands and raised her up,
And they saluted and cheered and praised her,
And when she fell upon them as a rotted corpse,
They healed her and bathed her and made her beautiful,
While she spat at them,
And ridiculed them,
And tortured them,
And murdered their children,
And stole their gold,
And all their lands,
And all their fortunes,
And all their souls.
And then they chewed their tongues,
And clawed at their faces,
And wished to die,
For they had all drunk the poisoned cup
Of the Wicked Maiden of the Upturned Star.

Sister Veronica
October 24, 2016

The Last Days

Our Savior puts His angels in
where humans fear to tread.

In this terrible and most distressing time,
The wall of the arrogant ones,
Which had been built up over the many centuries
Of their many and horrible successes,
Seemed almost, and frighteningly, impenetrable,
For even though they had been soundly defeated
In the first earth-shattering battle long ago,
The perpetrators of the most heinous
crimes (and there were all kinds)
Refused to accept the gleaming truth
That was shining in their faces on that fateful day
And continued along with their evil plans that had been
So carefully, so craftily, so deftly, and so insidiously laid.

Their secret fortress of doom and destruction
continued to stand tall,
Protected and defended by people who
didn't even know whose it was,
For if they did, they would be shocked
and fall down dead from fright.
No amount of humiliation, shame, penitence, remorse,
Nor fear of getting caught, would enter the blackened
hearts of the keepers of this evil edifice,
Or stop them from doing what they had long set out to do.

And so, after some weeping of the weaker ones,
And their rejuvenating blood-soaked bacchanalias all over the world,
And sacrifices to their odious horned and worm-eaten idols,
They set about setting fires and riots in the
streets, the spreading of disease,
Much more rape and pillage, reckless
abandon, destruction of all sorts,
And the most pernicious plots of mayhem and murder
they had ever tried in the history of their kind.

The good of this time, who knew of the Great Sufferer,
And who had also been suffering along with Him
This whole, distressful and seemingly unending time
(For the world was so connected at this time
That no one could ever say they did not know just how relentless
And villainous this terrible lot was and how far they would go
With their harmful, dreadful, and purposeful machinations),
Felt great sadness and perplexity at the situation.
They began to feel a sense of abandonment and fear
That all their efforts, and the constant risking of their lives,
Could still not break through the great Ring of Evildoers
That had taken over this most blessed Earth at this time.

But the Lord of all the realms,
And the great, and sometimes unfathomable, Holy Spirit,
Whom the native peoples of our planet knew well
(And whom the evil ones also knew well),
They, the Holy Family, who had given their own
Son, begotten of a loving Earth Mother,
In the great hope that their most recalcitrant children
Would melt their frozen hearts and change their bloody ways,
Had been hearing the pleas and cries and entreaties
of all those who loved them in their hearts

(Even though they sometimes didn't know
or understand them very well,
For there had been many obfuscations,
maligning and preventing of the truth),
And had indeed been suffering along with
them and watching their good exploits
This whole rotten and disgusting time.

But what these wicked and seemingly invincible people
(If one could even call them people, for they
truly were the dregs of humanity)
Did not know is just how many times
Our great and sometimes incredibly unfathomable Holy Spirit
Tried to rescue their souls and especially their bodies,
For souls and bodies were wedded together in human beings,
And so was their precious blood that should never be spilt,
Or used for any purposes other than saving a human life.
They also didn't realize that the Creator's Divine Light shines in
every person on the planet so that all could eventually see the
truth of things in times of great darkness, perfidy, and stupidity.

So, on the very last day, the Holy Spirit and the Father of All,
Who had long gotten fed up with all that was going on,
Decided to reveal to the world all the bad
deals and all the bad deeds
The wicked ones had wreaked on the earth behind the scenes
And expose all their abominations that had
been set up around the world.
All at once, the great Divine Light flashed
all over blessed planet Earth,
Turning over all the tables of those who
would harm their fellow man.

Each of the perpetrators of this great crime against humanity
Were immediately stripped of their power, and the
lights were turned off in their secret hiding places,
Which, since they were underground, were
now completely in the dark.
And since no one knew exactly where they
all were, they could not be rescued
And would lurk under the earth naked,
hungry, and afraid forevermore.

Sister Veronica
November 21, 2016
(Revised February 22, 2022)
(Revisited July 27, 2022)

Comes the Reaper

Comes the reaper for the weevils,
For they have ravaged both the wheat and chaff.
"Make the field a lake of fire!"

Comes the reaper for the weeds,
For the seedlings have been choked with lies.
"Cut them down where they stand!"

Comes the reaper for the seeds,
For they have long caused desolation.
"Open the pit and cast them in!"

And so, the sowers of the rotten crops
That had strewn abominations
In all the fields across the globe
Were sentenced to the darkest depths
And would walk the earth no more.

May God help them.

Sister Veronica
April 11, 2015

Red Flowers

To the Vovas and the Sashas
and all their grandfathers, fathers,
brothers, uncles, and sons

Weighed down by the medals on his chest,
And weary from the din of jets and parades,
An old soldier laid down his cane,
And sat on a bench in the sun.

The tanks had rolled by; the troops had saluted,
And many an honor was given in full,
When along came a very young little girl
With a bright red flower to offer him.

He couldn't see her standing in front of him,
But he knew she was there just the same.
And that quiet little moment—which made it all worthwhile—
Was the biggest celebration of the day.

May 9, 2015

On the seventieth anniversary of Russia's Victory
Day in the "Great Patriotic War"
May 9, 1945, to May 9, 2015

The Cell

To Pastor Saeed Abedini on his birthday,
incarcerated in Iran for being a Christian

"Remember my chains in your freedom!"
"Remember the sun on your faces," he cried,
As he sat out another birthday without his family and friends
In his dark and lonely cell in the middle
of the desert of a foreign land.

But the crowd outside was only hostile to his plight,
And drowned out his pleas and prayers with curses and mockery.
They became indignant against his exhortations,
And shouted at him with all their might.

"Let him rot with his Book and his prayers," they sneered.
"He's a proselytizer and a fool! He chose
to go there of his own free will."
"Beat him," they yelled. "He broke the law. May
his 'God' save him now!" they scoffed.
"Let him preach to the lizards and cockroaches."

But through the cruel taunts and damning chants
His voice rang out to them once again:
"My dear brothers and sisters, I am here of my own free will,
In this prison of pain and strife, but I pray
not for myself, but for you."

"Love one another," he implored,
"Don't imprison your bright lands in darkness and shackles.
Try to see the light,
Save your blessed peoples from my fate."

But they only grew more angry and violent at him,
And threw rocks and banged on the bars with sticks,
"Whip him again!" they demanded, "He's a criminal!"
And then cheered merrily when a thief was released in his place.

All at once, through the cheering and glee
At the release of the other prisoner,
A powerful and familiar voice rang out
Over the crowd:

"Remember my chains, my beloveds.
Remember the sun on your faces,
Remember the pure air you breathed so freely,
And the good foods you were blessed with."

And then suddenly, without any warning,
The sky turned blood-red and then black,
And a frigid wind swept up the sand up into heaps,
Instantly burying all who were standing on the outside of His cell.

Trapped in their permanent graves of darkness and ash,
They instantly awoke to a horrible consciousness:
They had no flesh and blood,
But yet they were hurting, hungry, and fearful.

And then all the mockers moaned and wandered in the dark,
"Let us out, save us, we are hurting and hungry!" they pleaded.
But their voices only returned an eerie echo to them,
And a stench of fire and brimstone filled the space they were in.

Then suddenly, a great rattling of chains began,
And the long, heavy steps of a visitor came toward them.
"Oh, you've come to save us, thank God!" they cried,
"God?" said the rather sinister voice.

"Oh, no, I'm not God," said the visitor.
"I've come to take you to *your* cells,
In the pit below, for you are criminals."
"But what did we do?" they cried anxiously.

"You mocked a great prisoner," said the visitor,
"You cast stones at Him and broke His law of your own free will,
So now you belong to me."
And so, all the mockers were locked up forever in darkness.

Starving, hurting, and lonely for century upon century,
They cried out for forgiveness with all their might,
But no one heard them in the din of celebration and bells,
For the sun had risen again and brightened
the troubled lands forever.

May 8, 2015
Sister Veronica
May the shining sun of the true Christ
Save and keep Pastor Abedini and his family.

My Son, My Son

Oh, my son, my son,
I am trying to reach you,
But you are up too high.

Here I am at the bottom of your world.
If I could, I would crawl upon the cross
And share the pain you bear.

Oh, my son, my son,
They've placed you up so high,
I can't reach you to comfort you.

Oh, my son, my son,
I can only wonder at the universe you see,
While I am here at the bottom of your world.

I was told I'd bear a son,
And that He would be the Son of God,
And now He is way up high.

Kim

To Kim Spierenburg

Sing for me, Kim!
Sing and play the violin for me!
You, who sit in pain,
Fly up and play for me!
You can walk in the clouds,
And swim in the wind,
And I will be praying for you,
For your beautiful voice,
And miraculous violin.

Cry of God

And when I heard His cry
It ripped through my soul,
For it was lonely and remorseful,
A doleful moan for His beloveds.
And I wished to comfort Him,
And beg Him for mercy,
And for one more chance to please Him—
So that He would not destroy this world.

December 1, 2019

Two Hawks

Two huge hawks flew over my head today,
Blocking out the sun for a moment.

They flew together toward the mountains,
Toward a snowy perch.

"No," one said, "Spring has not yet come to these parts."

"No," said the other,
"Nor has love."

March 19, 2020

Will You?

See me.

Dream of me.

Touch me.

Kiss me.

Take me.

Love me.

Need me.

Keep me.

Cir. 1990s

Your Captive

I am the essence.
You are the vessel.
Capture me.

Cir. 1990s

Shhh

Don't say sex,
Say love.

Don't say give,
Say take.

Don't say go,
Say stay.

Don't give up,
Give in.

Cir. 1990s

Sage Robber

I want to rob from you
The knowledge of the Universe.

I want to steal
All your meditations.

I want to purloin every facet
Of your beautiful mind.

I want to explore
Every crevice of your psyche.

I want to wander through your dreams
And rub against your thoughts.

I want to go down deep inside
Where no one else has been.

I want to be that close inside of you.

Cir. 1990s

Blood Brothers

Please don't go away to lick your wounds,
As mine are truly deeper.
My life force has spurted from me,
And now you are its keeper.

Take my blood, for I have no use of it,
If it cannot flow with yours,
And if this gaping hole's not filled,
Death shall take its course.

Cir. 1990s

China's Dream

Wall of Fate,
I am left outside.
Away my lover waits,
And so, the gap is wide.

But you cannot pen our dreams,
Nor strip away our thoughts that marry,
And if only by moonbeams,
Our love will always tarry.

Cir. 1990s

A Song for Auntie Olga

All of us look for her
Up in the sky
Now.
There she flies like the birds she loved so much,
Our loving mother, grandmother, aunt, and grand auntie,
Living her life just as brightly as she did on earth,
God's
Angel.

For Ms. Olga Elizabeth Every 1909–2009, RIP

On Human Cruelty

Jennifer
Entered heaven today.
Now she's gone,
No more torture
In this life on earth.
Friends have killed her.
Evermore her sweet spirit's free now.
Rest in peace, God's angel of love and kindness.

In loving memory of Jennifer Lee Daugherty, RIP

February 12, 2010

Mercy

"This Ebola outbreak is a scar on the conscience of the world."
—Liberian President Ellen Johnson Sirleaf, May 8, 2015

"No one would touch her," they said,
Even as tears streamed down her face.
And when her body shook with fear,
No one could comfort her,
No one would dare.
So, she leaned on a tree,
And waited her turn,
While her mother passed mutely away.

In honor of Mercy Kennedy
May 9, 2015

The Cage

To Pilot Muath Safi Yousef al-Kasasbeh,
burned alive in a cage in the bloody year
of 2015, RIP

What was that strange light I beheld in His eyes?
What heavenly power held His head up so high?
What impossible grace guided His stride,
As He slowly passed His masked accusers?

What did He survey in that vast barren desert?
What ancient markers did He see,
When He gazed so intently out there,
Beyond the obelisks and pyramids?

As He calmly walked to the cage of death,
He looked through the gloves and the masks,
Of the servants of the antichrist's hand,
While the true serpent slithered deeper in the sand.

In the bonds of a goddess defamed,
By the ash-filled apples of Sodom,
The entire earth stood still in thrall,
As Lucifer's minions lit the flames once again.

How many times has the Lamb been slain?
Under how many banners have they assailed His plan?
How many rotted idols have the fallen worshiped
Since the time they threw down His Holy Word?

Yet when the tongues of fire rushed to His feet,
He lifted His face and His hands in sympathy,
And with a plaintive wail to the watchers, He said,
"It's not me you are burning, my dear brothers."

Then when the divine essence of His body went up to the ether,
And the lumps of flesh and bones and ash
had gone back to the earth,
The blue sky suddenly clouded over and darkened,
And the crowd of masked men stood aghast in fright.

For as a chilly wind ran over the sands of Golgotha,
They all heard an ominous whispering:
"It's not me you have sentenced to everlasting darkness.
I had risen for your lives once, but now you are truly dead."

Sister Veronica

On the Painter Jeremias Gomez

As wretched and painful as his life has been,
Burned and scarred and misunderstood,
He has been privy to a shadowy, unfathomable but sacred realm:
Chaotic, multidimensional, spiritual, and cosmic—
As close to God as one can get on this earth
Without crossing over permanently.

And his paintings, adorned with rusted nails,
Street tar, melted crayons, Magic Markers,
nail polish, and assorted junk,
Are a fragile, precious record of that elusive secret kingdom
Which hides behind the lie of the outer eye.
How fortunate are we to have a glimpse of that forbidden zone,
Where Pablo, Vincent, and Leonardo roam.

June 19, 2015

Chloe

On that cool afternoon of an early autumn,
She picked for me sprigs of lavender—
My darling friend, my Chloe,
Her bent head determined quite seriously
To strip the bush of its pretty purple dress,
And yielding, in deference, it did bend for her.

And we walked on farther into the woods,
Farther and farther, deeper and deeper,
On trails carpeted for us by autumn's fervor,
Chloe's head bent quite seriously again
In choosing leaves for pressing,
"For my father."

And I offered her saffron, paprika-red and rusty pumpkin,
Which she refused as "still not good enough."
So, on we sailed in a fresh virgin sea of fall-shaken leaves,
Each one mute—heard only by the brightness of its color.
In patient anticipation, they lay in wait
To be chosen perchance by Chloe's slender, determined hand.

We did walk on still deeper into the woods,
Redolent in nature's green perfume,
And left its pretty tapestry quite trampled
By Chloe's determined feet
That crushed without a care
All but the most "perfect" leaves—for her father.

And it seemed to me we left those woods quite forlorn,
For as I looked back, its golden halls
Had mellowed to more somber tones:
Spent maroon, deep plum, burnt ochre, and smoky eggplant;
Its former beauty replaced only for a moment
By the flash of Chloe's long golden hair, "From my father."

Then out of the dusky woods and into the world walked Chloe,
With her treasure of fragrant lavender and precious leaves,
While the last rays of an overripe sun, a tarnished crown,
Remembered the radiance of Chloe's long golden hair
As she bent her head once again in determined examination
Of those carefully chosen leaves—for her father.

Mount Holyoke College Cir. 1997

Tatiana's Lament

To Alexander Sergeyevich Pushkin,
Russia's Shakespeare.

I am a person
Destroyed by life,
Destroyed by love,
Destroyed by you.

You were the sea to me,
You came to me in waves.
And now, I am in the desert,
In madness,
In emptiness.

Here nothing ever grows,
Nothing is created,
And even the earth
Can't breathe.

Flirting

B: "Well, I was a bad boy, but that's not the problem.
You know, flirting was a lot more fun
When I had someone to go home to."

E: "What?"

B: "She left me a note and her keys."

E: "When?"

B: "On Wednesday."

E: "It's over, B."

B: "But I love my wife."

E: "Forget it."

B: "You know, I wanted to kill myself this weekend."

E: "Don't be stupid."

B: "It took all of that to make me see that she's the one I really want."

E: "No further comment."

Beautiful and Just

Within this ring of atoms,
I am to thee wed.

You visit me, secret desire,
And your eyes are lonely.
Yet we cannot meet,
Never touch,
Only long for one another.

A kiss in the darkness,
Just one embrace,
Costs the soul so much.
This span reaches—
Can you cross over that bridge?

Side by side both gods live,
Each vanquishing the other.
Neither happy,
Never as happy
As the moment our eyes meet.

My soul wants you, it directs me,
My body and mind.
I could follow in the darkness,
Meet you at the chapel for a kiss.
No one prays anymore.

But they'll come, they'll see you.
Like Adam with the snake,
You're too visible in the garden.
You'll drag them with you,
Like the dust on the hem of your cloak.

Then you, in your tall beauty,
Will walk out in shame.
But they'll blame me,
And they'll say, "Look at her,
She sinned in church."

I could wear the stain, easily,
But you could not.
You have too many priests.
They'll want to absolve you of sin,
Take you in, burn me at the stake.

I could take the pain,
Bear the brunt for us,
But you wouldn't let me,
You'll want to follow.
I can't hurt them.

What shall we do?
We absolutely are, but cannot be.
Time will save us—it ticks out the answer.
It comes closer every day,
To tear this half away and then the other.

There is the irony that fate loves.
She sates her desire, but we cannot.
Now, burn these words, you must!
Leave no trace of our love,
For love should always and ever be
Beautiful and just.

For D and D, RIP
August 31, 1997

On the Death of William F. Buckley Jr.

Man, for some reason, subjects himself to tyranny:

First to tyranny of the one,
Then to tyranny of the majority,
Then to tyranny of the minority,
Then back to tyranny of the one.

Man, for absolutely no reason, subjects himself to tyranny.

February 27, 2008, RIP

Ode to Mirabai

Look, Dark One,
Look at what you have done to poor Mira,
She's all loneliness and pain,
Eyes hollowed out by tears for you,
White lips frozen in a drooping grin of
madness. She's skin and bones!
See what your dark power has done to your Mira.
Behold if you can the parts you once loved,
Withering away like abandoned apricots,
All their honey gone, wasted.
Mira's tree is dead without you.

July 7, 1999

To H and M

Sisters,
I still hear them giggling,
Still sharing
The very same thoughts—
Every old secret,
Renewed through Cheshire cat
Smiles.

February 28, 2005

The Birches

The birches, pale birches, lithe,
White on white,
Like flitting dancers
In the snow—
Their toes immune to the frost,
Their headdresses glistening
In a column of sun.

They dance in the wind,
Waving to the pines,
They bend and bow,
First, all together,
Then one by one,
All their pirouettes
Frozen in time.

Field of Blackbirds—a Song of War

My nation,
Your nation,
Their nation,
Our nations
Pecked to death
On the field of blackbirds.

My bridge,
Your bridge,
Their bridge,
Our bridges
Obliterated without a trace
On the field of blackbirds.

My land,
Your land,
Their land,
Our lands
Lived for, fought for, died for
On the field of blackbirds.

My monuments,
Your monuments,
Their monuments,
Our monuments,
Crushed to rubble
On the field of blackbirds.

My face,
Your face,
Their faces,
Our faces
Beaten and bloodied
On the field of blackbirds.

My children,
Your children,
Their children,
Our children
Afraid to play amongst the skulls and bones
On the field of blackbirds.

April 2, 1999

Saint Theresa and the Pope

To T. S. and her loving mother

Two wretched bodies,
Each one dying for their rights,
Rights to live as a young woman with food and water,
Rights to die as an old man in gold and purple.

I and you cannot decide,
Someone else will
Cut the ties that bind them to this earth.
Humanity is dead.

It's been seven days
And I see only one judge.
Victory is his,
On this day,
Good Friday.

Reaper, reap then,
Every day,
Every night,
Reap what you sow.

March 31, 2005, RIP

The NKVD

How lucky your soul is
To be so diligently guarded
By your conscience.
How perfectly it has welded and fitted
You to your wife, your work,
And your progeny.

Ever vigilant, it protects those large windows at the top of your face
Through which you once safely spied on me,
While looking at the others.

But you couldn't fool your conscience.
Like the NKVD, it caught the whims of your soul,
And then drove it away in its Black Maria.
Like the NKVD, it interrogated, imprisoned, and broke its bones
So that it can't even peek through the bars,
So that it won't ever speak those volumes again.

October 11, 2004

To the Lady of the Lake

With lilies, lions, and cortege,
You left the abbey at the edge:
Our hunted huntress was forced to pay
With hand and heart and life at bay.

Of common and uncommon love,
Their fear—you're stronger than the dove.
As angels heard your guardsmen step,
The queen did bow, while millions wept.

Above their heavy oaken burden
And past the castle's dour warden,
Your soul has soared to reach its den,
Where heaven reigns beyond our ken.

Like the lepers, you would often greet,
Came countless mourners to your feet.
A common flower flung from the crowd
Flew lightly past the heads that bowed.

Sapphire eyes that watched from pages
God has not dimmed but rendered ageless.
Without your prince and royals too
Came true love and homage due.

A sacred Oval marks the grieving Earth
Where nature's grace has filled a gaping dearth.
With some "magic dust," we'll break the spell,
From the pains of love, you'll now be well.

Beneath the glass, your spirit's free!
A Queen of Hearts, you hold the key.
And to give them light in tunnels dark,
All of heaven is your park.

The Bridge of Souls has led you home,
And never will you be alone,
While the oak and beech and willow weep
For our true princess at her sleep.

For Diana, Princess of Wales
RIP August 31, 1997

He's Home!

To my wonderful husband, Christopher

The cruel chuckle of giddy girls just off the school bus,
An embarrassed boy's soft retort,
The rude roar of an overhyped motorcycle,
A disturbed dog's warnings to a zooming FedEx truck,
The scratch of a pigeon's claws when
changing places on the lamppost,
A garrulous crow's mocking caws as he cuts
the wind with his sharp, black wings,
The buzz of busy bees in the neighbor's rosemary bushes,
The sun pouring out its two o'clock shine on the sidewalk,
Spa playing the touching strains of a lonely guitar over the Internet,
A rustled wind chime singing out a broken tune,
Jets piercing the peace of a heavenly blue sky,
Creepy the cleaner making his way across the pool,
The crackle of garlic and olive oil in the frying pan
Do not best the double vroom of a shiny red Subaru,
Pulling into the driveway to the heralding howls
Of happy puppies and a very happy wife.

January 25, 2012

A Prayer to Humanity

Oh, please, I beg you, my fellow humans,
Let us have no more war among us.
Let us end the devil's hecatombs now and forever.
Let us not serve his deceitful desires anymore.
Let us end his murderous parade of killers and victims.
Let us trust one another and depend on each other,
And face our true Creator with humility, integrity, and love,
And then may we reach for the stars.

Sister Veronica,
September 24, 2015
Münklingen, Germany

Bruised Love

To Misako M.
RIP May 4, 2005

Many people admired her,
In their eyes, she had everything,
So many didn't see the pain,
And the scars she hid in her heart.
Kindness covered them up.
Oh, if only we had known…

I Will Not Die for You Again

On the state of humanity in 2015

Oh, glorious human being!
You are my most perfect creature on this earth.
Why are you wallowing in darkness?
I don't recognize you anymore.
Your thoughts are lower than the beasts I put in your care.
What have you done to your shining soul?
Why has its bright light gone out?

I had such hope for you.
I loved you so very much.
I made you in my image.
I gave you paradise and everything you would ever need.
I gave you a mind and a soul that can outshine the sun!
What have you done to yourselves?
Why have you completely forsaken me?

After centuries of toil and warfare, you seem
to have learned nothing at all.
You are cunning, cold-blooded, and cruel.
You crave nothing but power and mammon.
A dog has more loyalty and integrity than you.
I am ashamed of my greatest creation.
Oh, you, covetous, vengeful, arrogant creature!
Why do you betray your fellow man and kill at will?

Reach down with your perfect and wicked hands,
Reach down through the rubble of your
empires of pain, dirt, and blood,
Reach down through the web of your lies,
betrayals, and ignominious conceit,
Reach down through the poisonous muck of
the insidious diseases you have spread,
Reach down through the broken buildings, burnt
bodies, and dry bones you've piled up,
Reach down through the dark depths of your
endless greed, selfishness, and depravity,
Reach down into the pit of darkness and eternal
fire and try to rescue your filthy soul.

Oh, you, pitiful, vain, and fallen human being!
My most perfect creature on this earth,
You have earned my wrath.
I implore you, spoiled children,
Repent and change your ways
Before I lose my patience and regret your very birth,
For I will not die for you again.

Sister Veronica
October 21, 2015

They Stoned Me...

To Farkhunda Malikzada
RIP March 19, 2015

They stoned me and burned me and threw me into the river,
My fathers, brothers, uncles, and cousins.

Six years on, they have cut off my feet and those of
My mothers, sisters, aunties, and cousins.

But why? This is the twenty-first century!
Why are you killing your family?

Lay the black tulips upon the sands,
No one will save them anyway.

2021

Tears for Damasak

To all the children of war

I am the skeleton that walks through your dreams,
And the flies on my eyes are your friends too.

I am poverty, death, and disease,
And the stench of the grave, it is there for you.

But we can remember the bones of the innocents,
And the cry of the little ones, lying in the dirt.

April 28, 2015

Because They Hated Freedom

They were free to come and go,
They were free to buy and sell.

Twenty years ago, there was a beautiful fortress
in the sky with two shining towers
That overlooked a large, happy city, filled with all kinds of people.
This bustling metropolis was a mecca of commerce and trade,
Where its people were free to come and go and
free to buy and sell as much as they wanted.

Then one day, twenty years ago, out of the blue,
when everything was going wonderfully,
Two vicious blackbirds flew into the towers, and in seconds
This mecca of commerce and trade, this bastion of freedom,
Was swiftly brought down to its knees, and all
who lived and worked there perished.

For twenty years, tears flowed, and hands were wrung
As to why the blackbirds had done such a terrible thing.
Some postulated jealousy, others revenge,
still others said it was sabotage.
But one young man, who had never seen his father,
stood up in his heavy chains and said,

"No. It's not because of any of those things,
it's because they hated freedom."

(On the twentieth anniversary of September 11, 2001)

Alfreda

Angels hovered 'round her youth,
Love came with a prince named Lawrence,
Friends leave their countries for her.
Receptive and gracious, she shares her home.
Each day is brightened by her smile.
December brought her good spirit to warm the earth,
And her name is Alfreda.

December 8, 2009

Catherine and Ben

Married in life,
Until the end of time,
Loved
Life
And Antigua.
Now they have been stolen from us.
Yes, we will remember them.

RIP August 3, 2008

But No One Heard Us

A plea from the souls of MH17

We were gliding peacefully through the clouds,
Without a care in the world,
When suddenly we were struck by a bolt from the blue.
When we looked out the window,
We saw flaming arrows,
And began to scream for our lives,
But no one heard us.

The pilots signaled
And sent out our distress call:
"Mayday, Mayday, we're all going down."
The mothers and babies cried,
The children squealed in their seats,
The men arose and roared at the sky,
But no one heard us.

So down we fell to the scorched summer earth.
After a while, some others joined us
And asked what we were doing there.
"We live here," we said.
"But you are dead," they said,
"Oh, yes, we're quite dead," we loudly replied,
But no one heard us.

"How did it happen?" the strangers asked.
"Our countrymen suddenly came to hate us,
And when we asked why, they killed us.
All winter we lay in the snow-covered earth,
Scattered in fields and strewn over houses.
We cried out in pain as the birds picked our bodies,
But no one heard us.

"There were arguments and accusations;
They blamed this one and that one.
There were conferences and committees,
And much wringing of hands.
There was tumult and mortars and war.
And our voices were muffled under the snow,
But no one heard us.

"Now the stench of death wafts over our graveyard,
Only the wind waves the flags of our past
Across the rotting field of deadly flowers.
One day, in May, we heard a dirge in the distance
And thought, At last, they are coming for us!
We shouted out, 'Yes, we are here!'
But no one heard us.

"Then as we lay alone in our grief, resigned to our terrible fate,
Along came some others out of the blue,
Who gathered around us and stayed by our side:
There were beautiful mothers and glorious fathers,
Bright children and wise grandparents,
And eager young students—all dressed up in white,
But no one heard us.

"They were walking and talking and grieving and wailing,
And we felt their great sorrow and pain,
But we could not console and comfort them,
For our souls lay in tatters on the cold, bare ground.
And we wanted to hear, 'Why don't you
leave us? You've all been set free.
Go to the light and enjoy your next life.'
But no one heard us."

Mercy for the victims of MH17 on that fateful day of July 17, 2014.
May the world hear your plea.

Sister Veronica
April 17, 2015

Children in the Crossfire of Donbass

To Kirill of Donetsk, age eleven

It was the year two thousand and fourteen.
Boys were playing football in the yard.
The sky was blue, and the sun was shining.
They were having the time of their lives.

They didn't know that their parents were arguing.
They didn't know that their neighbors were fighting.
They didn't know that their countrymen were separating.
They didn't know that there were shootings.
They didn't know that bombs were exploding.
They didn't know that rockets were coming...

It was the year two thousand and fourteen.
Boys had been playing football in the yard.
The sky was blue and the sun had been shining.
They were having the time of their lives.

November 6, 2014
Revisited March 10, 2022
(During wartime, yet again)

Curse of Sappho

Sappho, deep within me,
Haunting is your name.
Your heated blood still rushes
Through each and every vein.

My lover's kiss does not complete me,
Nor does he take my hand.
Ripe apples left not reaped
Burst forth upon the land.

The sweetest honey always lies
Deep within its comb.
The ripest peach is way up high,
But its nectar stays unknown.

We both fell in Hades,
And I live mine on earth—
To walk not amongst the Pleiades
But to seek what I am worth.

When I shed that ancient tear
And look from where you leapt,
I hold inside omniscient fear
That shows me why you left.

What led you to that plunge
Was cursed passion's flame.
Hold me back, dear Sappho, Sappho!
Lest your legend be my fame.

Cir. 1990s

Don't Leave Me Here...

Don't leave me here,
Not in the dark;
Don't douse the flame
But leave the spark.

Let's swim again in that warm old sea
And lose ourselves within its tow,
Tossed by the waves of ecstasy
Till our faces with its rapture glow.

I, who told you everything
That made your fires rage,
Am left alone to suffer for
Our sins upon this page.

Cir. 1990s

Little Dream

Away little dream,
Fly quickly to my lover's heart,
Let him ponder reckless passion
As I do when we part.

Careful, as you enter,
Do not disturb his blissful sleep,
But gently slip within my visage
For his mind to ever keep.

Cir. 1990s

The Shrouds of Rio

Let's pretty Rio, quick let's do!—
With sands of white and skies of blue,
With golden bodies baking true,
With jewels and roasts and mountain's dew.

To our dear home the Summit's come,
Where good men and women race
To save the earth! To save our children!
Oh, in what a more beauteous place?

Oh, in what a more beauteous place
Were children laid like logs of wood,
Full beautiful in childhood's face,
And sleeping silent, as they should.

And, oh, how silent is their slumber,
While we are free to flit about,
Together they are rolled like lumber,
Come, let's discuss the latest drought!

A festival with costumes,
And most of all with masks,
Oh, pretty, pretty Rio,
How gruesome is your task.

Cir. 1990s

Unfinished

The object of a woman's scorn,
The target of a man's desire,
Of these things I am truly worn,
As they try to douse my fire.

Full of passion and warmth I am
With no one fit with whom to share,
My soul floats lonely through its plan
When no one knows how much I care.

Dear God, you keep me day to day
From giving up my lifelong search,
You keep my downcast thoughts at bay
As I weep from my forsaken perch.

Sweet Prince, lover of my dreams,
I await in hope your coming.
So far away you are, it seems,
To you alone I am running.

Rescue me, oh, my darling sun,
I do not wish to live in pain.
Rescue me and make us now one,
For fear my life be lived in vain.

Cir. 1980s

Ares

God of war, you've slaughtered me
And left me here to die.
With a broken heart and loneliness,
I beg to ask you, why?

What deeds deserve such a heinous crime?
Have you never known a soft caress?
And has this caused your frenzied mind
To relish such duress?

Let me soothe your furrowed brow
And bring you to my heart,
For it's love you really need now,
And we should never part.

Cir. 1980s

301

The Worm May Turn

Compassion for the lowly ones
So often and so near!
Compassion for their haunting cries
Of lives so filled with fear!

Who then will render such a kindness
When the table's turned?
Who then will lend a hand, not blindness,
To those of us so spurned?

Cir. 1980s

Bloody 2015

Sit on your thrones, you wicked beasts!
And hear the wailing and screams in the streets.

Paint your offices with stolen gold,
And warm your palaces with blood-soaked oil,

For you do not care what havoc you wreak,
You do not care for the weak and the meek.

But the Lamb is sending His Heavenly Host
To avenge the blood that's been shed the most.

Sister Veronica
February 2, 2015

Shield

Oh, my darling Ares,
How you intrigue me so.
I want to give you everything,
But that you'll never know.

Yes, I want to taste your wildness
And touch your thumping breast,
But you must forgive my childishness,
As I suffer through this test.

Will you kiss me tenderly
When you've made your kill?
For from that moment on,
I'll no longer have my will.

Cir. 1980s

Hera

Let her cast her barbs upon you,
For you will not have to weep.
Put your face against my breast,
My heart is yours to keep.

I don't mind her prickly thorns,
For I know that this is true:
Here is where you'll always come,
For it is only I and you.

Cir. 1980s

Lovestruck

Cupid's arrow turned a dagger,
Left me nothing but a stagger.

But I'll soon get up and walk away,
For tomorrow is another day.

Cir. 1980s

Union

I am here vacillating
From the shock of love.
My heart is still pulsating,
As if a captured dove.

As you press your warmth upon me,
My insides start to melt,
A fire going through me,
Like this I've never felt.

Now you've stepped upon the threshold,
Plowing through my fret,
You've broken through so forceful,
There's no time for regret.

Firmly fixed together,
Culmination's done.
We stay attached forever,
For now we are as one.

Cir. 1980s

307

Cellmates

If loneliness is a prison,
Then may I share your cell?
And though we won't be christened,
We'll make a heaven out of hell.

Hearts safely tucked within the other,
We shall never be afraid,
And we'll live on this way forever
In this blissful world we've made.

Cir. 1980s

308

My Paris

Yes, fair Helen, I have my Paris,
But he cannot give chase:
My world does not allow desire,
And his fervor goes to waste.

But if Cupid shall pull on his bow,
And change my love's direction,
Then in his arms my heart shall glow
And know Elysium's perfection.

Cir. 1980s

Eye Talk

Whisper something warm and lovely
So that I know that you are near.
Fill me with sweet nothings
Till I'm beaming ear to ear.

Touch me beneath the tablecloth
And show me you are real,
For it's your touch I long for,
It's the way you make me feel.

Cir. 1980s

The Tower

The princess in the ivory tower,
Watching life go by,
Watches daily by the hour
And I often wonder why.

She looks so lonely way up there,
As if no one will ever reach her.
Does she not know that I do care
And soon I will release her?

Cir. 1980s

Flight of Icarus

Wings of passion set me free
And took me out of night;
They brought back that lover's plea
That launched an epic flight.

Ever higher did I soar
Amongst the clouds above.
Fed by love's delicious fire,
There was nothing to have fear of.

High into the clouds I sailed,
"Warn me not, for I am in love!"
"Tell me not the sorrows I have wailed,
For I am as lofty as the dove!"

"Let me never be earthbound!" I cried.
"Cold earth let my feet never touch!"
Ever higher and away I tried,
For I loved the sky so much.

Ah, what an exulting flight, I thought,
Joyous, precious, tempting fire.
In no net of fears would I be caught,
For I have heard Apollo's lyre.

I was deaf to admonitions,
Their pious clouds of gray.
I soared ever higher to the sun
To catch the brightness of this day.

But then at once my wings did fail,
And down I went, back to the earth.
Yet as I plunged, I did prevail,
For what is love but what it's worth.

Cir. 1990s

The Silver Bird

She was beautiful and full of grace
As I watched her soar each day.
Up in the sky, up into space,
I watched her fade away.

She was glorious and powerful.
She shined brightly in the sunlight.
The churned wind roared beneath her
As she vanished from my sight.

I watched her every day it seemed
And heard her thunder overhead.
Against the bluest sky she gleamed,
And to her journey off she sped.

I watched her once again this morning,
Her body strong and sleek.
Her presence gave no warning,
Not a wince to prove her weak.

Up she soared to reach the summit,
And I stood small and unaware,
When all at once I saw her plummet,
Stoically, without a care.

I thought the very earth did move
When it felt the force of her mighty breast.
She hit the ground she never knew,
But on now had come to rest.

Smothered hisses slowly waned
With the cries of those beneath her.
Blackening in the sun in pain,
I watched her writhe and wither.

I didn't understand the peril,
I thought I knew her well.
What had she ever done in this world
To deserve that instant hell?

Cir. 1980s

Love's Fire

I kissed fire, and it burned me,
And now I am afraid.
The scar it left upon me
Is a bed I've truly made.

What will ever keep my heart
From this enticing flame,
For the wounds that I will suffer
I have myself to blame.

Cir. 1980s

Caught

Snare me in your net, Hephaestus,
And show me to the world of eyes,
But you shall never know such passion,
Never be so wise.

You spy on me so piously,
As though you've never known such lust,
But, my darling, can't you see?
It's you I want, Hephaestus!

Cir. 1980s

To God

Oh, God, what scary destiny
Have you chosen here for me?
I await each day apprehensively
As to what my fate will be.

I pray to you each night
To keep me well and safe.
Could you find it in your heart
To spare this little waif?

And so, my good Lord spoke to me
In words of such perplexity:
"Oh, little waif, do not fret so,
For when it's time, I'll let you know."

Cir. 1980s

317

Carousel

Faster, faster goes this life
I call a carousel.
Around and around and faster still,
It's causing quite a spell.

More and more, and around again,
Until my ticket's out,
For when the music stops for me,
My ride on earth shall end, no doubt.

Cir. 1980s

Barbed Fire

I thought I could divorce you from my heart,
But now the barb of love is back.
You left a burning scar upon it,
For I've found it's you I lack.

Yes, I love you, and I need you,
But now this wound must heal.
So let us face this test together
To prove our love is real.

Cir. 1980s

The Prince

Don't give to me a bloodless kiss,
But grant me this my one sole wish:
That I might find my prince in you,
And need not search my whole life through.

Cir. 1980s

Erebus

Deep, dark Erebus,
Shall I ever climb out of your lonely depths?
This is a place for lost and loveless souls,
Where tears of hopelessness are wept.

But I want love, I want the sun!
I don't know how I got here.
Oh, let me go, and let me run
To love again—without my fear.

Cir. 1980s

Earth's Angel

Too much time in purgatory
Makes you withered, old, and gray.
I must break out, this world's too bleak
To face another day.

My sins, I wear like medals,
For they are all I've earned.
This flower lost her petals
Long before she learned.

Love, the greatest thief,
Steals from the mind as well.
It leaves you standing near
The gaping maw of hell.

When all I ever wanted
Was happiness and peace,
A child, a lamb, the same,
Innocence is fleeced.

I grow up so confused
And search for what is real.
Though you always look at me,
You can't know how I feel.

I reach for love, it burns me,
And so, I shy away.
Now it's back to purgatory
To serve another day.

Cir. 1980s

Lady of Sorrows

Lady of Sorrows,
You look down from the heavens now
Upon us, the transgressors of this world.

Your tears fall like pearls
Across your silken dress.
Your sacred heart beats with trepidation.

Oh, Beautiful Mary,
Your love for us is infinite,
As infinite as your only Son's.

Sister Veronica

The Blue Rose—an Ode to Mary Magdalene

To Anne Baring

Oh, Sister, He trusted you
With the Tree of Life itself,
And you anointed Him
For His Holy Journey.

Your towers stand together now
In the heaven of all heavens
Where Divine Sophia, the Virgin and God the Father
Watch over your children.

When we look out upon the Universe,
We see your glory and your kingdom,
One trillion million stars,
And one blue rose.

Sister Veronica

The Holy Blaze

To the caretakers of the sacred lands of the
United States of America.

Their Mask of Death was hung at every door,
Proudly and arrogantly.
Their frightening music played
Boldly and ferociously.
Their labyrinth of lies and spies tightly
Wove itself around every house
And every nook and corner.
The ground beneath them
Shook with terror
From the darkest depths.

They loved to mock and steal,
And we were tired of it.
We love to love,
And never tire of it.
They loved to bring harm,
Mayhem, and death,
And we would take it no longer.
Above all, they loved money,
And power,
More than the precious peoples of the earth.

And so, when the call to arms
Went out across all the sacred lands
To bring down the great Black Snake
That had sold its soul to the Dragon of Doom long ago,
We did not bring our thunder and lightning of old,

We did not scorch the earth and its moon,
For we were tired of wearing grief on our faces.
Instead, we called upon the Great Holy Spirit,
Who had long been watching the bane
Of the human race and the evil ones from afar…

When it was all over, and the earth had been purged
Of the great abomination that had plagued it for so many centuries,
We then linked arms with our long-lost
brethren, what was left of them,
And dressed them in coats of many colors, in shoes
of many dances, in flags of many dreams,
In the feathers of the many souls whose
bodies were removed from this earth
Without cause, without mercy, without love,
And bade them to listen to the chirps of joy on the wind,
To wipe the tears of the doves and the deer,
To renew the lost laughter of their children,
And to guard the sacred lands evermore.

Sister Veronica
December 5, 2016

You Will Listen When You're Dead

In the first quarter of the twenty-first century,
John the Baptist came to a street corner in London,
With a well-worn Bible in his hand
To preach the Word of God to passersby.

"Jesus is the Way and the Truth!"
He shouted as the crowd passed by.
"Jesus is the Way and the Truth!"
He shouted to all the passersby.

Then two policemen came up to him
And asked him to stop shouting.
They said that no one wanted to hear what he had to say,
And that he was disturbing the peace.

"I am not disturbing the peace!" cried John the Baptist,
"I am bringing the peace!—the peace of brotherhood and love."
But the policemen got angry and arrested him,
And took his Bible away from him.

And as they took him away in the paddy wagon,
John the Baptist kept on preaching:
"You will listen when you're dead!"
"You will listen when you're dead!"

October 7, 2021

Order of the White Dove

To the Moon Maidens of Sophia

We formed a magic circle,
Clasped hands together,
And then flew down from the heavens.

We came to this earth on a mission
To aid the creatures of this world,
To help assuage their sufferings.

The Holy Spirit, the White Dove,
Is our guide.
We do Her bidding.

But we found that She was cast out many moons ago,
Cast out from the temple on high,
And Her sacred groves were burnt to the ground.

Since then, this place has been ruled by the Dark One,
He keeps the worldlings in chains
And swords.

Now the Holy One's beautiful lands are stained with blood,
Her skies are black with soot,
And Her seas are poisoned.

We formed a magic circle,
Clasped hands together,
And then flew back to the heavens.

February 16, 2022

She Was Kind to Me…

To Monalisa Hood, RIP

She was kind to me,
My forever mother-in-law.

She gave me a brush for my hair
And a satin pillow to sleep on.

She made me a teepee full of presents,
And made sure I always felt loved.

She was a very special lady, a special mother, special grandmother,
And understood when I had to say goodbye.

Now I call on her sweet spirit in the heavens
When I am lonely and sad.

And I know that she still smiles at me,
And always wants the best for me.

She was kind to me,
My forever mother-in-law.

The Sacred Desert

I am at the bottom of a vast sea
That ran away from the earth a long time ago,
And now I bask in its hot golden sands
And sail along its endless highways.

I don't mind the sun. I don't resent him,
Even though I haven't seen an oasis in ages.
The sand snakes will lead us to water.
They never fail us. They are our brothers.

My caravan is small but hardy.
The rhythm of my camel is hypnotic.
He knows the way by heart.
He eats too many dates. I have spoiled him.

My mind winds to the far-off strains of the sacred duduk.
I dance in my dreams for the one I once loved.
He will never find me here,
My father made sure of that.

At night I see an ancient path in the ribbon of stars
That mirror each grain of sand in my hands.
I sleep soundly in the cool wind.
The jinn watch over me.

My elders told me the story of a Holy Man
Who crossed this way as a boy.
They say He is the Savior of the world.
He loved the desert too.

Soon I will see the mirage of the pyramids,
And the Nile will beckon and sparkle for me.
But my soul belongs to this barren place—
Where God breathes in secret.

Clothes from Europe, Secondhand

To the innocent victims in conflict.

We were sitting in the basement while the shooting was going on.
We had no food, no water, no heat, and no one to help us.
All I had left were my thoughts.

Who started this war? I wondered as I sat in the cold.
Who really started this war? Why are they killing us?
Why would they want to kill their brothers?

We were in a convoy with our children.
We tried to evacuate the danger zone.
We were waving a white flag to escape from the shooting.

But they caught up to us and took our white flag away from us.
They wouldn't let us leave the city, wouldn't let us get to safety.
We were kept as their prisoners, and they hid behind us.

Who started this war? I wondered as I sat shivering in the cold.
Who really started this war?
Why are we killing our brothers? Why are our brothers killing us?

I wanted to shout out, shout out my questions to the world,
But I was scared to death of being discovered.
All I had left were my thoughts, and no one could hear them.

Then they came into the basement and rushed us to the street,
And when they placed us in a line to form a human shield,
I caught sight of Lena's shop, "Clothes from Europe, Secondhand."

March 1, 2022

A Soldier's Prayer

Here I go again, God, on yet another special mission.
This time I go to fight my brothers,
Because they won't listen to reason.

How many sins will I rack up on my soul now, God,
When I have to go and fight my brothers,
Because they won't listen to reason?

Oh, if only we could embrace and make amends instead of wars,
For I truly love my brothers.
But we don't listen to reason.

March 1, 2022

A Message from Marina

To Ukraine, Russia,
and the innocents of war.

I got a message from Marina,
Who was sitting in the basement of her apartment building,
Where she was hiding from the gunfire
And bombs on the streets:

"I haven't eaten for days, and there is nothing to drink.
I'm so cold, and I haven't taken a bath.
I feel so dirty. Pray for me."
And that was the last time I heard from her.

So I warmed myself, ate some food, drank
some water, and took a bath.
I washed myself with sweet-smelling soap,
Shampooed my hair and doused myself with perfume—
And then prayed for Marina.

March 1, 2022

The Judas Coin

Blessed are those who wash their robes, that
they may have the right to the tree of life and
may go through the gates into the city.

—Revelation 22:14 (NIV)

It was a time of great peril in the latter
part of the eighteenth century
When a mighty king ruled his island country with an iron fist.
Men repressed each other and killed one another.
No one could speak up against the status quo.

But some stood up against this tyranny
And rebelled against repression
And crossed the seas to seek a new way of living,
A way very different from the status quo.

However, the king soon got wind of this,
And sent his armies across the seas
To seek out and crush those who wanted freedom,
Those who wanted more than the status quo.

After a savage, merciless battle, those who
rebelled finally won their freedom.
They then wrote up a precious and sacred document
To ensure certain inalienable rights, one of which
Was the right to speak up against the status quo.

Then came the twenty-first century, and the
world was once again in great peril.
But when it came time to speak up against tyranny and repression,
Those who had long enjoyed freedom suddenly looked
the other way and took the Judas Coin instead.
They then destroyed the precious and sacred
document—all to preserve the status quo.

Sister Veronica
March 23, 2022

The Flying Whales

The world was on the brink of disaster.
Everyone had their missiles pointed at one another.
Mutual annihilation was assured.
It was just a matter of who would press the button first.

Tensions were mounting, tempers were lost,
And there was no amount of negotiations
That could resolve the differences
That had been simmering for centuries.

But just when the moment of destruction
Was going to be irreversibly and fatefully launched,
And the end of humanity was in the offing,
Suddenly a strange and wonderful thing happened:

All at once, without any warning, all the airplanes
that were in the skies at the time
Began landing right where they were flying.
They landed on the sea, and they landed on the land,
Gently and smoothly without any harm to anyone.

Once the skies were cleared,
All the whales in all the seas about the earth
Began jumping into the sky!
One after another, they leaped straight up to the clouds.

Then each one took its place in a great spiral
That stretched across the earth,
From north to south and east to west,
From the North Pole to Antarctica, from Russia to America.

They then began to change colors in midair,
Some were pink, and some were violet.
Some were orange, and some were green.
Some were even rainbow-colored.

Around the earth, they glided gently in the air,
These enormous heavenly creatures.
They made their way over the continents first
And then countries, then cities and towns,
and especially over war zones.

Everyone was astounded at the sight
And stopped what they were doing at the time.
Some were amazed, and some were a little frightened,
But all looked up and stood in wonder at
what was happening in the sky.

When they had formed a braided chain around the whole planet,
All the whales began to sing their whale songs.
Oh, what a marvelous sound this was,
Joyful and a bit sad at the same time.

They formed a great chorus of melodies and harmonies
No one had ever heard on the earth before.
This amazing music penetrated the very hearts of people
In ways they never thought possible.

The voices of the whales were so beautiful and sonorous
That everyone forgot their troubles
And immediately sat down to listen to the wondrous chords
Whose vibrations caressed every part of their mind, body, and soul.

Oh, what a wonderful feeling this was!
People began laying down their weapons.
Tears started to flow, embraces followed,
And hands were warmly held.

Then when everyone was at peace, all the
whales started to leave the skies
And soar higher into the atmosphere.
Up, up they went, one by one, effortlessly and gracefully,
Stationing themselves right at the edge of space.

Soon the whales formed a great circle above the planet.
The clouds had parted, and the weather was so perfectly clear
That all could still see them floating high above,
Smiling sadly and singing now mournfully, now joyfully.

At that moment, people all over the world looked at one another,
Perplexed by the heavenly miracle
That had taken place on this fateful day,
For now, there were no more whales on the earth.

What would happen now? they thought. How
could we ever get them to come back?
And then the wonderful feeling they had
been experiencing started to fade,
Replaced by a great sadness and a terrible sense of loss,
A loss never felt before and never felt again.

2022

The Purple Pyramid

They had only come once to the earth,
Those who landed in the purple pyramid
In a blazing violet fire that didn't burn.

What a day that was for the humble human race.
Yes, they were humble then and stood in awe
At what God had sent them from above.

These people from the sky were very beautiful,
And had skin tones of many hues and varied features,
As they were from many different cultures around the universe.

As soon as they introduced themselves,
They set about sharing the marvelous gifts
They had brought with them from far distant galaxies.

They taught their various languages, literature, mathematics,
Astronomy, arts of all kinds, dancing, singing,
And many more things too numerous to name.

They taught the people how to grow crops and cook delicious foods,
How to sew decorative garments, how to keep their bodies healthy,
How to use the metals of the earth to make tools
and adornments that never tarnished.

They taught the earthlings how to build wonderful homes,
Schools, orchards, gardens, exquisite buildings,
And comfortable coliseums for gatherings, games, and fellowship.

They showed them how to channel the energy of the earth
To bring light into their dark huts with crystals and tall obelisks,
And how to guide their vessels across the
seas by the sun and starlight.

Before they left the earth for good, these kind and loving people
Built three huge pyramids set in a lush oasis, guarded by a great lion
That pointed the way to their homeland among the stars.

Each of these enormous edifices was faced
with gleaming white marble
That shimmered in the sun and was topped with a golden capstone
Whose shining light reached all the way
out into space, like a silver cord.

One day, the people from the purple pyramid decided
to return to see how the earthlings had fared
In the many long centuries they had been gone.
When they tried to land, however,
The earthlings destroyed their vehicle with a missile,
and they were never heard from again.

2022

The Jaded Soldier

It's so hard to carry my gun now, God.
It gets heavier every day.
I can hardly lift it up anymore.

One day, I won't be able to lift my gun at all.
One day, I'll have to put it down for good.
One day, I won't even have a gun.

March 31, 2022

The Loneliest King in the World

To Vova

There once was a king of the largest country in the world,
A country so vast, so wide that it spread across
the earth like a sprawling ocean.
Now this country had seen a lot of strife.
It had taken many centuries to put it all together.
To unite so many cultures under one flag is not an easy thing to do.

Although it would seem a good thing to gather
together so many different nations,
The peoples of this country did not always get along.
Many resented being part of a huge conglomerate.
They wanted their own country,
Their own way of life.

Then there were the outsiders,
Always seeking ways to break up this enormous empire.
To this end, they were always invading the outlying areas,
Always trying to trespass the borders,
Always trying to influence the citizens to rebel.

And rebel they did, the citizens of this vast country.
First, they set up their own borders
Around what they thought were their own lands.
Then they wanted their own language that
no one else would understand,
And they wanted their own customs and ideas.

This would also seem a good thing, this idea of self-determination,
That people could have the freedom to
think and do what they wanted.
But then they became divided once again and began
to fight one another in their own lands.
They fought each other so ferociously, so viciously, so vindictively
That soon there was no one left standing in
the once-vast country but the king.

March 31, 2022

Bloody Easter 2022

He had given His life for us more than two thousand years ago.
He had risen to look after us from heaven.
He left us with the Book of Love
To show us the way to the path of perfection.
But we didn't follow His Word.
We covered the earth in blood and wounded,
We made war instead.

So, once again,
We have forced a crown of thorns on His head,
We have scourged Him,
We have nailed Him to the cross,
And driven a spear into His side,
Because we don't follow His Word,
We make war instead.

Sister Veronica
March 17, 2022

I Threw My Soul to the Wind...

I threw my soul to the wind,
  And someone saw it.

I threw my heart to the sky,
  And someone caught it.

I threw myself to the world,
  And someone found me.

Oh, how I love that someone.

About the Author

Elena Veronica Hall was born in San Jose, California. She graduated cum laude from the Russian Language and Cultural Studies Program at Mount Holyoke College, South Hadley, Massachusetts. She holds certificates in the study of the Russian language and cultural studies from the Russian Language Institute at Bryn Mawr College, Bryn Mawr, Pennsylvania; the Russian State Pedagogical University in Saint Petersburg, Russia; and the Moscow International University, in Moscow, Russia, furnished by the American Council of Teachers of Russian (ACTR).

Mrs. Hall worked as a legal secretary until her late thirties. After gaining her associate in arts degree, cum laude, at Miami Dade Community College, she then pursued her bachelor of arts degree at Mount Holyoke College—Frances Perkins Program. She has traveled widely throughout her life and has lived in the United States, the Netherlands Antilles, Puerto Rico, Russia, and Germany. She has studied Spanish and French and is considered fluent in the Russian language. She now lives in Sierra Vista, Arizona, with her husband and three Jack Russell terriers.

CPSIA information can be obtained
at www.ICGtesting.com
Printed in the USA
BVHW041510050523
663654BV00005B/78